Recent Themes in Military History

Historians in Conversation:
Recent Themes in Understanding the Past
Series editor, Louis A. Ferleger

Recent Themes in

MILITARY HISTORY

Historians in Conversation

Edited by Donald A. Yerxa

THE UNIVERSITY OF SOUTH CAROLINA PRESS

© 2008 University of South Carolina

Published by the University of South Carolina Press
Columbia, South Carolina 29208

www.sc.edu/uscpress

Manufactured in the United States of America

17 16 15 14 13 12 11 10 09 08   10 9 8 7 6 5 4 3 2 1

Library of Congress Cataloging-in-Publication Data

Recent themes in military history : historians in conversation / edited by Donald A. Yerxa.
    p. cm. — (Historians in conversation. Recent themes in understanding the past)
   Includes bibliographical references.
    ISBN 978-1-57003-738-2 (cloth : alk. paper) — ISBN 978-1-57003-739-9 (pbk. : alk. paper)
    1. Military art and science—History. I. Yerxa, Donald A., 1950–
   U27.R3485 2008
   355.009—dc22

2007050822

This book was printed on Glatfelter Natures, a recycled paper with 50 percent postconsumer waste content.

Contents

Series Editor's Preface

The Historical Society was founded in 1997 to create more venues for common conversations about the past. Consequently, in the autumn of 2001, the Historical Society launched a new type of publication. The society's president, George Huppert, and I believed that there was an important niche for a publication that would make the work of the most prominent historians more accessible to nonspecialists and general readers. We recruited two historians who shared this vision, Joseph S. Lucas and Donald A. Yerxa, and asked them to transform *Historically Speaking* into a journal of historical ideas. Up to that point, *Historically Speaking* had served as an in-house publication reporting on the society's activities and its members' professional accomplishments. Yerxa and Lucas quickly changed the layout and content of *Historically Speaking,* and within a short period of time many of the most prominent historians in the world began appearing in its pages—people such as Danielle Allen, Niall Ferguson, Daniel Walker Howe, Mary Lefkowitz, Pauline Maier, William McNeill, Geoffrey Parker, and Sanjay Subrahmanyam. Historically Speaking's essays, forums, and interviews have drawn widespread attention. *The Chronicle of Higher Education*'s "Magazine and Journal Reader" section, for example, repeatedly has highlighted pieces appearing in *Historically Speaking.* And leading historians are loyal readers, praising *Historically Speaking* as a "must-read" journal, a "*New York Review of Books* for history," and "the most intellectually exciting publication in history that is currently available."

The Historical Society is pleased to partner with the University of South Carolina Press to publish a multivolume series, Historians in Conversation: Recent Themes in Understanding the Past. Each thematic volume pulls key essays, forums, and interviews from *Historically Speaking* and makes them accessible for classroom use and for the general reader. The original selections from *Historically Speaking* are supplemented with an introductory essay by Donald A. Yerxa along with suggestions for further reading.

Louis A. Ferleger

Acknowledgments

As editor of *Historically Speaking* since 2001, I have accumulated considerable debt to an amazingly talented and diverse group of scholars. This volume illustrates well the extent of my debt. It has been both a pleasure and an honor to work with many of the finest military historians and military analysts in the world. Several historians whose work appears in this volume have contributed multiple pieces to *Historically Speaking* over the years. These include Andrew Bacevich, Max Boot, Niall Ferguson, Victor Davis Hanson, Dennis Showalter, and Jeremy Black. Jeremy, in particular, has been an editor's godsend, willing to contribute provocative pieces in timely fashion on a variety of topics.

I would especially like to mention my ongoing gratitude to Clark G. Reynolds (1939–2005), scholar, mentor, and friend.

Introduction

The Curious State of Military History

Donald A. Yerxa

The public's appetite for military history seems insatiable. Publishers churn out books on all aspects of military history, not a few of them making it to the best-seller lists. Military history is the staple of cable television's History Channel and is featured in series like Fox News's "War Stories" hosted by Oliver North. And, of course, war movies attract major box-office attention—for instance, *Braveheart* (1995), *The Thin Red Line* (1998), *Saving Private Ryan* (1998), and *Hotel Rwanda* (2004).

Yet the status of military history in the academy is precarious—at least according to a number of recent commentators. To be sure, classes in military history generally enjoy robust enrollments. But according to John A. Lynn's 1997 jeremiad, "The Embattled Future of Academic Military History," the academy is an increasingly hostile place for military history. Faculty slots in military history are being lost to trendy approaches to the study of the past. The reasons for this, Lynn contends, are varied but include military historians' avoidance of theoretical complexity, the overwhelming maleness of military historians as a group, and the simplistic linkage in many people's mind of military history with right-wing foreign policy.[1] Victor Davis Hanson and Robert D. Kaplan echo much of Lynn's lament.[2] But while Lynn suggests that military historians would do well to recognize that subfields like gender history and particularly the new cultural history offer "interesting new possibilities," Hanson argues that military history provides a corrective to the nonsense he believes infects a good deal of history produced by academic historians. He is upset that students are exposed to "new takes on race, class, and gender in the Civil War" while the fact "that millions were freed only through the military excellence of Union armies and their leaders" so frequently goes without mention in the college classroom. "If one really does wish to learn of the important events of the past, one then needs to know something about war," Hanson states unapologetically. "One book on World War II is worth ten on the history of fashion; a class on the Peloponnesian Wars is more valuable than fifty on the rhetoric of gender."[3] Kaplan, a top journalist, criticizes the guild for failing to appreciate the many virtues of military history. These include its general disdain for philosophical abstraction, its relevance to policy makers, its appeal to the general reader, its realistic assessment of human nature, and its centrality to broader historical understanding.

Military history's uncertain status in the academy continues to generate debate. In the fall of 2006, John J. Miller updated the case for the decline of academic military history in a *National Review Online* piece, "Sounding Taps: Why Military History Is Being Retired."[4] Miller argues that military history is either dead or under siege at most of the top universities in America. In those institutions where it still has a foothold, military historians have had to distance themselves from traditional operational history—the kind of military history that focuses on the details of how battles unfold—and embrace an approach that explores the cultural aspects of war and military establishments. Miller observes that at Princeton University, the University of Michigan, and Purdue University, faculty slots once held by military historians were lost upon retirements. And at the University of Wisconsin–Madison, he claims, an endowed chair in military history remains vacant because of the history faculty's reservations about the field. A number of historians have challenged Miller's analysis of the situation, none more forcefully than a distinguished group of military historians at the Ohio State University. They made a compelling case that military history is flourishing at OSU and that strong programs exist at places like Duke University, the University of North Carolina, Texas A&M University, and Kansas State University. Rather than whine about censorious political correctness, they recommend that military historians become better "ambassadors for their field."[5]

While Miller's blanket report of military history's demise in the academy is possibly overstated, the relatively few institutional exceptions to his assessment tend to support his case. What makes this debate so interesting is that from an intellectual standpoint, military history is quite robust, as the various offerings in this anthology attest. The following pieces, drawn from the pages of *Historically Speaking* from 2002 through 2007, were written by very prominent military historians and analysts. This volume makes no claim to be representative of the entire field of military history with its vast literature. There is little focus on traditional operational history or the history of specific wars—a future volume in this series will do that. Rather, this volume highlights a few important themes in recent military history that reveal its intellectual vitality and its valuable contribution to overall historical understanding.

One of the most significant trends in military history is the so-called cultural turn. This general approach to military history is influenced to varying degrees by cultural anthropology and represents a challenge to those who view war primarily as a rational, purposeful, instrumental political activity. The influential nineteenth-century Prussian military thinker Carl von Clausewitz famously argued that war is "a true political instrument, a continuation of political intercourse, carried on with other means."[6] But those who have taken the cultural turn in military history consider the Clausewitzean view "incomplete" and "parochial." According to John Keegan, "War embraces much more than politics. . . . It is always an expression of culture, often a determinant of cultural forms, in some societies the culture itself."[7]

Although culture can be a slippery conceptual tool with limited explanatory power if used indiscriminately,[8] the value of the cultural approach to military history has been demonstrated repeatedly. It sheds light not only on the impact of war on culture but also on the role of culture in shaping military activity. One need go no further than two recent books with fundamentally differing theses—Hanson's *Carnage and Culture* and Lynn's *Battle*—to appreciate the value of the cultural approach. Hanson selects "landmark battles" that illustrate various aspects of the "Western way of war" thesis. He contends that there has been a "peculiar practice of Western warfare . . . that has made Europeans the most deadly soldiers in the history of civilization."[9] For Hanson culture matters, and it can be demonstrated in the bloody business of decisive battles. It matters no less for Lynn, but he wants to avoid generalizing patterns that advance what he describes as stereotypes of Western and non-Western warriors and ways of war.[10]

The cultural approach has provided a catalyst for comparative military history. While there is much more work needed to investigate the military history of many parts of the world in order for a mature comparative cultural approach to emerge,[11] the "Western way of war" debate points in the direction of world history. Whether military history needs to be decentered—as some would argue it should—or simply expanded to include the non-Western world, it is clear that many military historians take an expansive view of the past. And their interpretations have become utterly integral to our overall understanding of the past. There is, of course, more to history than wars and battles, but one cannot hope to comprehend the past, especially in broad brushstrokes, without coming to grips with humanity's military experience.

In January 1955 Michael Roberts delivered his inaugural lecture, "The Military Revolution, 1560–1660," at the University of Belfast. Roberts argued that the changes wrought by firearms and the tactical reforms of Maurice of Nassau and Gustavus Adolphus led to larger, more disciplined, and more expensive standing armies. Supporting these armies necessitated bureaucratic mechanisms that led to more centralized and complex governments. Put simply, late sixteenth-century tactical reforms helped to bring about the modern nation-state. Almost as soon as it was published in 1956, Roberts's thesis was incorporated into accounts of early modern military and political history. In 1976, however, Geoffrey Parker modified the original formulation of the military revolution by calling attention to the importance of siege warfare in the sixteenth century. The fortifications developed to resist artillery assault first in Italy and then all over Europe were the real keys to the military revolution and were ultimately responsible for the increased size of European armies. In 1988 Parker expanded the concept of the military revolution to include naval warfare and the experience of European militaries in colonial settings with the publication of *The Military Revolution: Military Innovation and the Rise of the West, 1500–1800.* The overseas expansion of Europe, Parker argued, was primarily a function of its superior armies and fleets. The military-revolution debate continued through the 1990s with Jeremy Black and Clifford J. Rogers, among others, contributing major critiques.

The military revolution debate wonderfully illustrates the importance of the military to overall historical understanding. In its bare essentials, this debate centers on whether advances in research and technology led to a military revolution in early modern Europe that in turn played a crucial role in the rise of the West.[12] No one has done more to advance the military revolution thesis than Geoffrey Parker, and the opening section of this anthology considers his important historiographical interpretation and its implications for contemporary military policy. Supplementing this forum is an interview of Max Boot, whose 2006 book *War Made New* examines military revolutions from 1500 to the present.

Military revolutions, or revolutions in military affairs as such major transformations are more often called, are at the heart of a heated debate in contemporary military circles. What is the place of technology in warfare? Have high-tech weapons systems—smart bombs, stealth bombers, global positioning satellites, and the like—effected another revolution in military affairs, rendering lessons drawn from military history antiquated? The harsh realities of American military involvement in Iraq and Afghanistan have certainly given ammunition to those who think history and culture matter as much as military hardware. The importance of military history to current policy debates is obvious in the forum that occupies the middle section of this anthology. Military analyst Colin S. Gray uses military history and his understanding of Clausewitz to predict that the nature of war—as opposed to its specific character—will not change in the coming century. A who's who of military analysts responds.

Another major trend in military history is the study of the experience of war and combat. This approach has its origins in the so-called new military history of the 1970s and 1980s. Embarrassed by the conceptual thinness of drum-and-trumpet military history, academic historians embraced war-and-society studies built on social science models. Instead of accounts of battles and biographies of military leaders, the new military historians wrote about things like logistics, the financing of war, raising armies, civil-military relations, and the demographic effects of war. So successful was this approach that some worried that warfare and battle would become peripheral to the field.[13] But while the new military history was rendering the study of war virtually bloodless, Keegan wrote his classic, *The Face of Battle*.[14] This was an attempt by a historian who had not experienced war himself—indeed, could not for medical reasons—to explore what it was like to be involved in a few key battles. Keegan's work spawned another genre of military history related to the new military history but with a decidedly unique focus: the experience of war and soldiering. One of the best practitioners of this type of military history is Richard Holmes, who has completed a trilogy on the British soldier. Part 3 includes an interview with him, along with an essay by Eric Bergerud accounting for the exceptionally violent fighting in the Pacific Theater in World War II.

As Robert Kaplan noted, military history is important because it offers a realistic assessment of the human condition. The wars of the twentieth century, particularly World War II, provide the historian with an abundance of source material for how humans reacted in desperate and violent circumstances, in victory and defeat. Two well-known British historians explore these matters in recent books: Max Hastings in *Armageddon,* his graphic account of the last months of the war in Europe, and Niall Ferguson in his *War of the World,* an impressive and depressing look at the twentieth century as "an age of hatred" and particularly at World War II, "the greatest man-made catastrophe of all time."[15] Part 4 consists of interviews with Hastings and Ferguson in which, among other things, they speak to the human condition in horrific circumstances.

This volume concludes with brief comments on the state of military history by Jeremy Black, one of the most prolific historians of our time. In several books and essays, Black has urged military historians to reconceptualize their craft, especially along global lines.

Collectively the contributions to this anthology—indeed, recent military history as a whole—reveal two important general themes. Military history is not just about the engines of war. It is tempting to assume that weaponry and the means to produce it define warfare through the ages. But people, cultures, and context really do matter. Most current military historians adamantly resist technological determinism. More important, recent military history reveals how integral war is to the broader understanding of the past. This is not to advocate for a naïve, triumphalist military historiography in which the past is essentially reduced to its military dimensions. History is too rich and complex for anything so simplistic. But any attempt to understand the past without taking war into account is flawed. As Max Boot argues in his book and interview, the outcomes of key battles really have changed history. Unfortunately, that appears to be an underappreciated in today's academy.

NOTES

1. John A. Lynn, "The Embattled Future of Academic Military History," *Journal of Military History* 61 (October 1997): 777–89.

2. Victor Davis Hanson, "The Dilemmas of the Contemporary Military Historian," in *Reconstructing History: The Emergence of a New Historical Society,* ed. Elizabeth Fox-Genovese and Elisabeth Lasch-Quinn (Routledge, 1999), 198–201; Robert D. Kaplan, "Four-Star Generalist," *Atlantic Monthly* (October 1999): 18–19.

3. Victor Davis Hanson, "The Return of Military History?" *National Review Online*, www.nationalreview.com, July 3, 2002.

4. John J. Miller, "Sounding Taps: Why Military History Is Being Retired," *National Review Online*, www.nationalreview.com, October 9, 2006.

5. OSU Military History Program [Mark Grimsley, John F. Guilmartin Jr., Geoffrey Parker, Jennifer Siegel], letter to the editor, *National Review,* October 7, 2006; reprinted in "Blog Them Out of the Stone Age" http://warhistorian.org/wordpress/index.php, October 7, 2006. Also see Allan R. Millett to John J. Miller, "Phi Beta Cons: The *Right* Take on Higher Education" (a *National Review* blog) October 26, 2006, http://phibetacons.nationalreview.com/post/?q=YzRkMTFkMzEzYzgwYmI5 MWRhMzMyM2JlZTg4MzNiOGQ=. According to OSU's Mark Grimsley, those who really care about military history should help fund the chair in military history at Wisconsin, which he argues is underfunded ("Care about Military History? It's Time to Ante Up," *Blog Them Out of the Stone Age,* December 5, 2006).

6. Carl von Clausewitz, *On War,* trans. and ed. Michael Howard and Peter Paret (Princeton: Princeton University Press, 1976), 87.

7. John Keegan, *A History of Warfare* (New York: Knopf, 1993), 12, 24.

8. See John Shy, "The Cultural Approach to the History of War," *Journal of Military History* 57 (October 1993): 25.

9. Victor Davis Hanson, *Carnage and Culture: Landmark Battles in the Rise of Western Power* (New York: Doubleday, 2001), 5.

10. John A. Lynn, *Battle: A History of Combat and Culture* (Boulder, Colo.: Westview, 2003), xvi–xvii.

11. Jeremy Black, "Determinisms and Other Issues," *Journal of Military History* 68 (October 2004): 1227.

12. Geoffrey Parker, "Military Revolutions, Past and Present," *Historically Speaking* 4 (April 2003): 3.

13. Paul Kennedy, "The Fall and Rise of Military History," *Military History Quarterly* 3 (Winter 1991): 11.

14. John Keegan, *The Face of Battle* (New York: Viking, 1976).

15. Max Hastings, *Armageddon: The Battle for Germany, 1944–1945* (New York: Knopf, 2004); Niall Ferguson, *The War of the World: Twentieth-Century Conflict and the Descent of the West* (New York: Penguin, 2006), xxxiv.

PART 1

Military Revolutions, Then and Now

Military Revolutions, Past and Present

Geoffrey Parker

A couple of years ago, a friend and I were cruising the shelves of London University's magnificent bookstore, Dillons (now merged into Waterstones), in which "History" occupied an entire floor. After passing "World History," "European History," and "Women's History," we lingered over "Military History" (reassuringly large) and then found ourselves in front of some shelves labeled "Black History." "Oh no!" my friend exclaimed. "Not an entire section filled with Jeremy's books!" Jeremy Black has certainly been prolific. He has 213 entries to his credit in the current bibliography of the Royal Historical Society. In the summer of 2002, one of his students hosted a party for him, entitled "Convergence," to mark the fact that the number of books he has written equals his age. Several of them deal with military history in general and a few with military revolutions in particular. Most recently, in *War: Past, Present and Future,* Black argues that military revolutions are *not* driven by research and technology, as some of us had supposed, but rather stem primarily from "military organization": "'Organization' can be understood in a double sense: first, the explicit organization of the military—unit and command structures—and second, organization as an aspect of, and intersection and interaction with, wider social patterns and practices, leading to the social systematization of organized force."[1]

Black criticizes historians like me who have argued that an important military revolution, based on technology and research, occurred in early modern Europe. On the one hand, he claims, we fail to offer empirical research, instead "employing individual cases as illustrations more than evidence"; on the other, he dismisses early modern Europe's Military Revolution as a chimera. While acknowledging that "Europeans created the first global

From *Historically Speaking* 4 (April 2003); © Geoffrey Parker, 2003. Reproduced by permission of Greene & Heaton Ltd.

empires" in the sixteenth and seventeenth centuries, Black denies that these empires were the fruits of a "technologically driven Military Revolution." Furthermore, he even denies that these empires exercised military dominance over the rest of the world's peoples.[2]

These denials overlook three important developments that took place between 1500 and 1650. First, superior military technology and combat effectiveness enabled relatively small groups of Spaniards to dominate thousands of square miles of Central and South America; second, those same assets enabled equally small groups of Russians to create the largest state on earth; finally, several groups of Western Europeans achieved mastery over the world's oceans thanks to a lethal combination of "guns and sails" devised by shipwrights along Europe's Atlantic coast.[3]

I contend that a military revolution did occur in early modern Europe, that it reflected advances in research and technology, not "military organization," and that it played a crucial role in the rise of the West. To avoid the accusation of "employing individual cases as illustrations more than evidence," I will consider here just one aspect: the emergence of infantry volley fire in the Dutch Republic in the 1590s. It was unquestionably an innovation based on technology and research, which Europeans later used to deadly effect to vanquish their foes overseas, and it also demonstrates the extent to which military revolutions "import" discoveries made by civilians.

Volley fire was invented twice in the sixteenth century: first in Japan and then in the Dutch Republic. The first Portuguese visitors to Japan in the 1540s brought with them some arquebuses, guns fired from the shoulder. They arrived during a period of civil war that had fragmented the archipelago into dozens of competing states. The local warlords therefore immediately saw the advantages in adding a powerful new weapon to their arsenals and ordered their metalworkers to make Western-style arquebuses. But muzzle-loading weapons, although superior to the bow in stopping power, suffered from a major problem: they were slow to reload. In the 1560s Oda Nobunaga, one of the warlords struggling for control of the archipelago, found a way around this problem: he realized the advantage of drawing up his troops in lines, so that the first rank fired a volley and then retired to reload while succeeding ranks followed suit, a procedure that would become known as the *countermarch*. In 1575 Nobunaga deployed three thousand men in ranks to deliver volleys with devastating effect at the battle of Nagashino. For the next fifty years, hand-held firearms became the most important infantry weapons in Japanese armies. Gunnery schools sprang up, many of them producing illustrated manuals for marksmen, which taught samurai how to shoot straight from various positions. After the 1630s, however, Japan "gave up the gun": the government confiscated all firearms and stored them in arsenals.

Could Europe have got the idea of the countermarch from Japan? Nobunaga entertained many Western visitors, and military conversation, with Westerners among others, formed one of his principal passions. Although no known Western source mentions the Japanese countermarch, this is merely absence of evidence, not evidence of absence. The discovery of just one document in, say, the Jesuit Archives in Rome, in which a missionary described the Japanese countermarch, perhaps plus evidence that someone in Rome mentioned it to a soldier, would transform the picture. It would not, however, prove that *the Dutch* learned the technique from Japan because its genesis in the Netherlands clearly lies in another source—a long letter written to Count Maurice of Nassau by his cousin, William Louis, on December 8, 1594.[4]

The letter discusses the use of ranks by the soldiers of Imperial Rome, as summarized in the *Tactica* attributed to the Byzantine Emperor Leo VI; then it lists the German or Dutch equivalents for thirty-four Latin commands used in drilling those ranks given in another book about classical Roman warfare, the *Tactica* of Aelian. Finally, William Louis addresses Aelian's long chapter on the countermarch. Of course, Aelian only discussed the maneuver using spears and javelins, but William Louis, in a crucial leap, realized that the same technique could work for men with firearms:

> I have discovered *ex evolutionibus* [a term that would eventually be translated as "drill"] a method of getting the musketeers and others with guns not only to practice firing but to keep on doing so in a very effective battle order (that is to say, they do not fire at will or from behind a barrier . . .). Just as soon as the first rank has fired, then by the drill [they have learned] they will march to the back. The second rank, either marching forward or standing still, will then fire just like the first. After that, the third and following ranks will do the same. When the last rank has fired, the first will have reloaded, as the following diagram shows: these little dots [*stippelckens*] show the route of the ranks as they leave after firing.

William Louis, like his cousin Maurice, had studied at Leiden University with one of Europe's foremost classical scholars, Justus Lipsius, whose *Six Books on Politics,* published in 1589, included an entire section on how rulers could learn from the wars described by classical authors. Lipsius saw the infantry as the battle-winner of his own times, as it had been for Rome, and argued that modern infantry must learn to operate in smaller units (like Roman "maniples"), to drill with their arms in unison, and to march in step, just as Roman armies had done. The very next year, 1590, William Louis began to implement these suggestions. According to his secretary, "He began to follow the precepts he found in classical texts . . . and drew up his regiment accordingly, making long and thin units instead of great squares and getting them to form and reform in various ways."[5]

In 1595 Lipsius published a book devoted entirely to the Roman way of war: *De Militia Romana*. It included a whole section on drill, with many quotes from classical authors. The Plantin press of Antwerp printed fifteen hundred copies and sent several of them to the northern Netherlands, either as gifts or purchases. One copy reached Maurice of Nassau, and according to a Dutch friend of Lipsius, Maurice's "only pleasures" while on campaign that summer were reading *De Militia* and "drilling his troops frequently."[6] Within four years, according to a contemporary, "New recruits to the army assemble two or three times a week to learn how to keep rank, change step, wheel, and march like soldiers." Maurice himself often took part, "and if a captain did not give or understand the right command, His Excellency told him and sometimes showed him" how to do it properly.[7]

Maurice next reorganized the Dutch infantry in order to make the new drills more effective. He reduced unit size, as Lipsius had recommended, and he increased firepower. Each infantry company now included thirty musketeers, with forty-four more armed with arquebuses and only forty bearing pikes. Furthermore, Maurice standardized those firearms. After extensive tests, he distributed five "model" muskets and five "model" arquebuses to various arms producers in Holland and decreed that henceforth all muskets must be made to the same design and must all fire a ball of the same caliber.

Meanwhile, in 1607 Count John of Nassau (William Louis's brother) published *The Exercise of Arms for Arquebus, Muskets, and Pike, as Ordered by His Excellency Maurice Prince of Orange*. Unlike the Japanese manuals, which emphasized marksmanship, *The Exercise of Arms* showed, step by step, how a soldier should handle his weapon in unison. A brief introduction provided the words of command, followed by 117 striking engravings in folio format. The musket sequence, for example, broke down the process of firing and reloading into forty-two separate positions, each with an illustration to facilitate mass imitation. Dutch and English editions appeared simultaneously; translations into Danish, French, and German soon followed.

No sooner had the Dutch army mastered drill, the countermarch, and volley fire than the techniques spread to other European armies. Apart from the various editions of *The Exercise of Arms*, several other books spread the word. John Bingham, an English soldier serving in the Dutch army, appended to his translation of *The Tactiks of Aelian* a special description of "the exercise of the English in the service of the . . . United Provinces of the Low Countries." Plagiarism, a hallmark of military history then as now, also played a part. A Frankfurt printer, Wilhelm Hoffmann, published *Instructions for Soldiers in Three Parts,* in quarto format, containing cheap woodblock copies of de Gheyn's elegant copperplate engravings; while the *Art of War for the Infantry* by Johan Jakob von Wallhausen, commandant of Danzig (now Gdańsk) in Poland, provided 130 pages of description to accompany composite images of de Gheyn's illustrations.

The Dutch also spread their innovations by personal instruction. Starting in 1610 many German Protestant states requested and received Dutch drill sergeants to teach their militaries, and in 1616 Count John of Nassau opened a military academy at his capital, Siegen, to educate young gentlemen in the art of war. Training at the *Schola Militaris* took six months, and students received arms, armor, relief models, and other instructional aids. They learned only the Dutch system.

The Dutch even instructed their non-Protestant allies. In 1649 the Republic supplied the engraved copperplates for a Russian translation of Wallhausen's *Art of War for the Infantry,* commissioned by the tsar, who presented a copy to every colonel in his army. It was only the third secular work ever published in Muscovy. According to a foreign ambassador, from then onward Dutch officers in the service of the tsar drilled veteran cadres "almost daily, because they must remain capable of training the others who are to be enlisted."[8]

By then the Dutch way of war had also spread to America. In the ruins of Flowerdew Hundred, Virginia, one of the earliest English settlements along the Chesapeake Bay, archaeologists have found a medal depicting Maurice of Nassau. No doubt it belonged to Sir George Yardley, one of Maurice's companions-in-arms and admirers, the first owner of the settlement who served twice as governor of Virginia. He was not alone: *every* governor of Virginia between 1610 and 1621 had served as an officer under Maurice. Indeed, the Virginia Company in London actively recruited Englishmen serving in the Dutch army. Many leaders of other English colonies had also served in the Dutch army, including Thomas Dudley in the Caribbean and Miles Standish at Plymouth (where men began drilling in the Dutch fashion as soon as they disembarked from the *Mayflower* in 1620). A decade later, in Massachusetts Bay, John Winthrop entrusted each of the colony's four militia companies to the veterans of the Dutch army whom he had persuaded to join him.

Today the enthusiasm of the Dutch for spreading their military innovations seems surprising. Boeing does not currently offer build-your-own-stealth-bomber kits or send out salespeople to demonstrate how the United States makes smart bombs, even to its allies. But the current climate of "obsessive military and industrial secrecy" (to quote Holger Herwig) is relatively new. At most times in the past, research, technology, and even patents readily crossed frontiers. To take just a few examples from early in the last century: in 1900, Chinese Imperial infantry killed German colonial troops with Mauser rifles; in 1902, Venezuela met German intervention with Krupp guns; most spectacular of all, in 1905, the Japanese navy annihilated a Russian fleet at Tsushima with ships and guns made in Glasgow and Newcastle.

An even more striking example of the open transfer of ideas and technology occurred in the 1930s. Throughout that decade, military experts as well as scientists kept a close watch on the dramatic developments made in atomic physics around the world. Nothing was concealed. In March 1939, as Hitler's forces entered Prague, Niels Bohr at a meeting in Princeton admonished the scientists trying to conceal their research to create an atomic chain reaction that "secrecy must never be introduced into physics." Scholars of all nations continued to publish their research, and so German, Soviet, and Japanese atomic physicists eagerly awaited the arrival of the *Physical Review,* which contained information about the latest American research into creating chain reactions with uranium, right down to the issue dated June 15, 1940—the day after the German army occupied Paris.[9]

The "openness" that prevailed in military and naval research and development during the first half of the twentieth century was a consequence of its complexity. No single mind, no single group could master all of it. There could have been no atomic bomb had the U.S. government not listened to a multitude of gifted if eccentric scholars from around the world— British, Danish, German, Italian, Polish, and above all Hungarian, as well as American—each with their own expertise and speaking a variety of arcane scientific languages. The success of the Manhattan Project depended not only on a huge financial investment but also on the participation of experts in mathematics, chemistry, physics, ballistics, aerodynamics, engineering, metallurgy, and so on, drawing initially on research by potential enemies as well as by presumed allies.

The complexity of modern science reflects two distinctive, probably unique, Western traditions, and they bring us back to Jeremy Black's thesis. First, research and technology have exercised an unusual influence on Western warfare because the West has normally lacked a numerical edge. Its enemies—from the Persian Wars in the fifth century b.c. down to the Gulf War in the twentieth century and the current Afghan campaign in the twenty-first century—have almost always enjoyed marked numerical superiority. This has repeatedly forced the West to invest heavily in research and technology in order to create force multipliers and, whenever possible, force equalizers.

The second distinctive—probably unique—Western tradition is that this research and technology is remarkably broad based. It depends upon understanding, controlling, and exploiting the perceived regularities and irregularities throughout nature to create a broad background knowledge that expands in a path-dependent, sequential way. This enables individuals to formulate questions and eventually to come up with answers in many different fields of inquiry. The shared background knowledge has included many components over time—some science but also (particularly in the early modern period) some pseudoscience, some history, some belief in supernatural forces—and these components have normally determined which discoveries were made. "Discoveries," because the shared background knowledge among many practitioners means that discoveries often occur in clusters and become self-reinforcing. Cultures lacking that broad base will still make scientific advances, but those advances will tend to be (in the phrase of Robert Merton) "singleton techniques." "Singletons" are normally discovered by chance, "and while their impact can at times be significant, further refinements and adaptations tend to be limited and soon run into diminishing returns."[10] This perhaps explains why the Japanese countermarch remained a "singleton technique" and why Japan "gave up the gun" once the civil wars came to an end.

The dependence of the Western way of war (to use Victor Hanson's elegant phrase) on science and technology normally involves two important trade-offs. First, crucial developments require time and persistence. It took over two decades to implement the countermarch (from 1594, with William Louis's "*stippelckens*," to 1616, when the States-General mandated the tactic for all infantry units). Likewise it took eleven years to develop the atomic bomb (from July 4, 1934, when Leo Szilard patented the idea of an atomic chain reaction in London—specifying that one of its consequences would be an "explosion"—until August 6, 1945, when "Little Boy" exploded over Hiroshima). All the components of the current "revolution in military affairs" (a phrase coined by the Pentagon's Office of Net Assessment) have been present for decades—satellites, tactical computers, and tactical missiles since the 1960s; e-mail and smart weapons since the early 1970s—but the military feared to integrate them into a system until the collapse of the Soviet Union ended the nuclear threat (at least temporarily) in 1989. It is still a work in progress.

The second important trade-off for Western warfare's heavy dependence on research and technology is the need it creates for extensive civilian involvement. As Andrew Krepinevich has noted, "Technologies that underwrite a military revolution are often developed outside the military sector, and then 'imported' and exploited for their military applications."[11] The history of the countermarch, of the atomic bomb, and of "stealth warfare," indicate that the best way to achieve a military revolution is for governments to encourage experts from all backgrounds to contribute and share their ideas on a broad range of disciplines for as long as possible.

Naturally the military remains suspicious of such openness, and favors instead the current climate of "obsessive military and industrial secrecy." Many if not most members of the United States armed forces today display a strong anti-intellectualism, doubtless rooted in the immeasurable harm done to them by Robert Strange McNamara and his "coterie of civilian whiz kids" during the 1960s. For much the same reason, many if not most members of the United States armed forces today also display a strong antipathy towards the politicians who seek to interfere in what they do. Nevertheless, in the words of Georges Clemenceau, who led France to victory in World War I, "War is too important to be left to the generals."

In his brilliant book *Supreme Command,* Eliot Cohen shows how leaving the conduct of war to the generals has rarely produced lasting victories.[12] He also reveals how, contrary to the received view, successive U.S. administrations since 1965 did precisely this. They failed to pick the right generals, they failed to conduct a strategic and operational dialogue with them, and they failed to set priorities and maintain proportion in what were, after all, secondary conflicts. In short, the politicians lost sight of what they needed to do to run a war.

Cohen argues that wars are won first by mobilizing civilian expertise and then by creating what he calls an "unequal dialogue" between the military and their political masters. Regarding the first, he notes that victorious wartime leaders in the past have listened not only to their military advisers but also to linguists, not only to defense analysts but also to philosophers, not only to rocket scientists but also to historians. Yes, historians. Remember that the reintroduction of drill originated with the Justus Lipsius. Remember, too, that Count Alfred von Schlieffen derived his celebrated "double envelopment" strategy from reading Hans Delbrück's vivid account of the battle of Cannae in his *History of the Art of War within the Framework of Political History,* published in 1900. Finally, remember the impact of Barbara Tuchman's *Guns of August* during the Cuban Missile Crisis. On October 13, 1962, Chester Bowles, the president's special envoy, asked the Russian ambassador in Washington if he had read the book (and when Dobrynin said, "No,"

Bowles proceeded to summarize the first few chapters). Two weeks later, President Kennedy told his brother Bobby, "I am not going to follow a course which will allow anyone to write a comparable book about this time, *The Missiles of October*." ("If," he added wistfully, "anybody is around to write after this.")[13]

Cohen also regards as essential a dialogue between politicians and generals in which "both sides expres[s] their views bluntly, indeed, sometimes offensively, and not once but repeatedly." But the dialogue must remain "unequal, in that the final authority of the civilian leader [is] unambiguous and unquestioned." All four of the war leaders examined in *Supreme Command*—Lincoln, Clemenceau, Churchill, and Ben-Gurion—gathered and digested pertinent information from all available sources, including civilian experts (many of them foreigners), and used it to fashion a stream of inquiries, probes, and suggestions to all those involved in the war effort. Although they seldom overruled their generals on a military issue, each of the four leaders became a world-class nag. Each won his war.

If the famous four were alive and in charge today, as the United States stands poised to wage another Gulf War, perhaps their nagging questions to the Joint Chiefs of Staff would run along these lines. First, since previous attempts to eliminate determined enemy forces by aerial bombardment alone have failed (most recently in Kosovo and Afghanistan), why does the Pentagon believe it will work now in Iraq? Second, since all history books show that it is better to go to war supported by allies rather than alone, why does the United States push its technological edge so far ahead of everyone else that even its NATO allies now find it difficult to fight alongside? Finally, because history teaches that military expenditure in peacetime never suffices for all military goals, the famous four might ask why the United States pours money into creating a missile shield of dubious efficacy, against a remote possibility, rather than teaching more of its troops the guerrilla, linguistic, and intelligence skills required to deal more effectively with the alarming rise of immediate high-concept, low-tech threats?

Our political leaders should learn from history—and from historians such as Cohen—and consult far beyond those empowered by the current revolution in military affairs. Victory in war comes not from superior military organization but from superior research and technology, not from hectoring and bluster but from listening and learning, not from blind acceptance of the parameters laid down by the military but from probing the military relentlessly on what they are doing and why. Naturally, the unequal dialogue will not endear the politicians to their senior military advisers. It did not endear the famous four to theirs. As Sir Alan Brooke, chairman of the Chiefs of Staff, wrote of Churchill in his diary two months after D-Day, "Never have I admired and despised a man simultaneously to the same extent." Churchill would not have cared. Another senior officer, who apologized after disagreeing "very forcibly" with a proposal from the prime minister, reported that Winston just smiled and said, "You know, in war you don't have to be nice, you only have to be right."[14]

NOTES

1. Jeremy M. Black, *War: Past, Present and Future* (New York: St. Martin's, 2000), 28–29. Admittedly Black includes in his definition of military organization "the systematization of knowledge, such that it is possible better to understand, and thus seek to control, the military, its activities and its interaction with the wider world." But the examples he offers are statistics and mapping, not the acquisition of knowledge through research.

2. Black states, "Historians who argue for a technologically driven Military Revolution as the key causative factor behind the European rise to dominance in the early modern period are mistaken, because, first, although the Europeans created the first global empires, this was only partly due to the military developments of the military revolution and, second, there was no European dominance" (*War* 95).

3. Black specifically discounts two of these important anomalies: "It is possible to consider the Spanish *conquistadores* as unique, and in addition, to regard the trajectory and causation of naval success, both in the Indian Ocean and elsewhere, as separate" (*War* 110). Possible, perhaps, but it seriously undermines the argument that no Military Revolution occurred in early modern Europe.

4. William Louis of Nassau to Maurice of Nassau, Groningen, December 8, 1594, draft: Koninklijke Huisarchief, The Hague, Ms A22–1XE-79, in W. Hahlweg, *Die Heeresreform der Oranier und die Antike. Studien zur Geschichte des Kriegswesens der Niederlande, Deutschlands Frankreichs, Englands, Italiens, Spaniens und der Schweiz vom Jahre 1589 bis zum Dreissigjährigen Krieg* (Berlin, 1941; reprinted Osnabrück, Germany: BiblioVerlag, 1987), 255–64; and W. Hahlweg, *Die Heeresreform der Oranier. Das Kriegsbuch des Grafen Johann von Nassau-Siegen* (Wiesbaden: Veröffentlichungen der historischen Kommission für Nassau, 1973), 606–10.

5. Justus Lipsius, *Politicorum sive Civilis Doctrinae Libri Sex. Qui ad Principatum maxime spectant* (Leiden, 1589), book 5: 13; Everhart van Reyd, *Historie der Nederlantscher Oorlogen, begin ende voortganck tot den Jaere 1601* (Leeuwaarden, 1650), 161a.

6. Justus Lipsius, *De Militia Romana libri quinque. Commentarius ad Polybium* (two parts, Antwerp, 1595–96); Raphelengius to Lipsius, August 29, 1595, in Jeanine de Landtsheer, ed., *Iustus Lipsius Epistolae* (Brussels: Koninklijke Vlaamse Academie van Beligë voor Wetenschappen en Kunsten, 2004), 513–17. Maurice commissioned a French translation of Lipsius's book; John of Nassau made a lengthy summary in German.

7. Arend van Buchell, *Diarium 1560–1599,* ed. G. Brom and L. A. van Langeraad (Amsterdam: Werken uitgegeven door het Historisch Gezelschap gevestigd te Utrecht, 1907), 3: 470, entry for July 1598; Kees Zandvliet, ed., *Maurits prins van Oranje* (Zwolle, The Netherlands: Waanders, 2000), 251.

8. Ambassador Karl Anders Pommerenning to Queen Christina, Moscow, *Riksarchivet, Stockholm, Diplomatica: Muscovitica* 39 unfol., November 7, 1649, on drilling Colonel van Buckhoven's regiment. On the *Uchen'e i khitrost' ratnago stroeniia pekhotnykh liudei,* see Richard M. Hellie, *Enserfment and Military Change in Muscovy* (Chicago: University of Chicago Press, 1971), 187–88.

9. See Richard Rhodes, *The Making of the Atomic Bomb* (New York: Simon and Schuster, 1986), 294, 311, 327, 346–47, 350.

10. Joel Mokyr, "King Kong and Cold Fusion: Counterfactual Analysis and the History of Technology," in *Unmaking the West: "What-If?" Scenarios That Rewrite World History,* ed. Philip Tetlock, Ned Lebow, and Geoffrey Parker (Ann Arbor: University of Michigan Press, 2006).

11. Andrew F. Krepinevich, "Cavalry to Computer. The Pattern of Military Revolution," *National Interest* (Fall 1994): 39.

12. Eliot Cohen, *Supreme Command: Soldiers, Statesmen, and Leadership in Wartime* (New York: Simon and Schuster, 2002).

13. "Report of Conversation with Ambassador Dobrynin on Saturday, October 13 [1962]," *U.S. Department of State, Foreign Relations of the United States, 1961–63. 11 Cuban Missile Crisis* (Washington, D.C.: U.S. Printing Office, 1988), 26–28; Robert F. Kennedy, *Thirteen Days: A Memoir of the Cuban Missile Crisis* (New York: Norton, 1969), 105.

14. Cohen, *Supreme Command,* 98, 128.

On Diversity and Military History

Jeremy Black

G eoffrey Parker correctly draws attention to our different views on early
modern warfare, ones I have discussed in *European Warfare, 1494–1660*
(2002), but I suspect there are more fundamental differences that repay consideration. I am wary about metanarratives and cautious about paradigms,
monocausal explanations, and much of the explanatory culture of long-term
military history. My emphasis is on diversity and on being cautious in adduc-
ing characteristics and explanations. Thus, in the series of books that accompany *War: Past, Present and Future—European Warfare, 1494–1660* (2002),
European Warfare, 1660–1815 (1994), *Western Warfare, 1775–1882* (2001),
Warfare in the Western World, 1882–1975 (2002), and *War in the New Century* (2001)—there is a stress on diversity within both the West and the Rest.

I am also wary of the idea of a Western way of war unless it is accompanied by due notice of the variety of contexts and taskings involved. There
was a variety of military cultures and practices within the West, although
the diversity is even greater outside the West. As far as Hanson's work is concerned, the attempt to draw continuities between an account of a particular
type of warfare in the classical period and the situation more recently would
benefit from an informed discussion of the Middle Ages.

More troubling than the underplaying of diversity within the West has
been the tendency to simplify the non-West. In terms of military cultures
and environments, the range was immense. Furthermore, this played a role
in the Western failure to exercise military dominance over much of the
world's populations, although other factors, not least the degree of Western
commitment, were also important. Rather than simply repeating the standard account of Western successes, it is worth considering the reasons for
European military failures in Africa prior to the nineteenth century, as well

From *Historically Speaking* 4 (April 2003)

as the problems encountered in East and South Asia. The bulk of the world's peoples were not in the New World. Deep-draught European ships found it difficult to operate in inshore, estuarine, and riverine waters, and here the major changes in force projection did not occur until the nineteenth century.

In the space made available, I cannot pursue this theme, but, alongside a number of other scholars, I am troubled by the deficiencies of the dominant account. I have tried to express my views in *War and the World 1450–2000* (1997), *War: An Illustrated History* (2003), and the editorial introductions to *War in the Early Modern World 1450–1815* (1999) and *War since 1815* (2003). This interpretation also relates to my "late-onset" series, most obviously *Eighteenth-Century Europe* (2nd ed., 1999) and *Europe 1550–1800: A Revisionist Interpretation* (2003), in which I have suggested that many of the characteristics attributed to modernity can better be dated to the nineteenth century than to the construct of an early modern period.

As far as military history is concerned, I am unhappy with the tendency to "demilitarize" military history seen with the so-called new military history of the 1960s and indeed have recently written *World War Two* (2003) in refutation of the Joanna Bourke approach. Instead, I welcome the current interest in the operational approach to conflict. As far as assessing capability is concerned, I am wary of any monocausal interpretation and am particularly unhappy about explanations focused on resources and technology. Mechanization plays a major role in the modern concept of war. There is a focus on the capabilities of particular weapons and weapons systems and a belief that progress stems from their improvement. This stress on the material culture of war can also be seen in discussion of earlier eras. Thus, with, for example, the Iron Age replacing the Bronze Age, the emphasis is on how the superior cutting power of iron and the relative ease of making iron weapons led to a change in civilizations. Weaponry is certainly important, but as we know from observing modern conflicts such as the Vietnam War and the Russian attempt to dominate Afghanistan, it is not always the best armed that prevail.

Instead I would focus on how resources are used, with all this means in terms of issues of fighting quality, unit cohesion, leadership, tactics, strategy, and the like, as well as with reference to the organizational issues that affect the assessment and use of resources.

Yet, to focus solely on battle for a moment, there is another problem stemming from the assumption that the "face of battle," the essentials of war, are in some fashion timeless, as they involve men being willing to undergo the trial of combat. In practice, the understanding of loss and suffering, at both the level of ordinary soldiers and that of societies as a whole, is far more culturally conditioned than any emphasis on the sameness of battle might suggest. At the bluntest of levels, the willingness to suffer losses varies, and this helps to determine both military success and differences in combat across the world in any one period. To contrast the willingness of the Western powers to suffer heavy losses in the world wars, especially World War I, with their reluctance to do so subsequently and also the different attitudes toward casualties of the Americans and the North Vietnamese in the Vietnam War is to be aware of a situation that has a wider historical resonance. It is far from clear that variations and changes in these "cultural" factors should play a smaller role in the history of war than weaponry. Morale remains the single most important factor in war. War, seen as an attempt to impose will, involves more than victory in battle.

Organizational issues—how troops were organized on the battlefield, the nature of force structures, and the organization of societies for conflict—also vary greatly. Instead of assuming that these were driven by weaponry, specifically how best to use weapons, and maybe also to move and supply them, it is necessary to appreciate the autonomous character of organizational factors and their close linkage with social patterns and developments. A parallel case can be made with the causes of war. Looked at differently, armies and navies are organizations with objectives, and in assessing their capability and effectiveness, it is necessary to consider how these objectives changed and how far such changes created pressures for adaptation. In short, a demand-led account has to be set alongside the more familiar supply-side assessment that presents improvements in weaponry or increases in numbers without adequately considering the wider context.

Tasking is very important in terms of force structures. This owes a lot to policies. Fundamental issues of social organization are also at stake in tasking, for example, the degree to which internal policing is central to military purpose. It tends to be underrated in conventional military history.

There has recently been a greater willingness to consider the implications of Nazi ideology for the purposes and conduct of the German military in World War II. There is also need for a much more systematic consideration of how ideological assumptions led to counter-insurrectionary and policing policies that affected other militaries. This was (and is) a dynamic process within countries and at the level of empires. In the case of the latter, the willingness to accommodate and indeed to acculturate to the more powerful, especially conquerors, has been far from constant across history. In general, the availability of syncretic options, for example, the assimilation of local religious cults by the conqueror's religion and the cooption of local elites, have been the most important means of success.

My ideas have developed over the years, and I can spot differences in emphasis in my work. On the whole, however, I have remained consistent in emphasizing diversity within both the West and the Rest. I admire Geoffrey's range and engagement with the subject and feel that his work has been fruitful in ideas. There is, however, no closure to this subject. Instead, there is a need to encourage research in a number of fields that have been relatively understudied, for example, the military history of Southeast Asia and the "Horn" of Africa and the problem of how best to develop analytical concepts that do not treat the world as an isotropic surface but, instead, make sense of different military goals and traditions. Imposing our concepts on purpose and conflict risk leading us to failures of judgment, which, as Parker correctly points out, have policy as well as scholarly implications. There will remain military and political limits to effective force projection, and skillful policy-making will continue to require a shrewd understanding of capability and limits. This is not new. Great powers found it necessary to learn and adjust to their capabilities and limits. The Mongols could not conquer Japan or Java, the Ming could not dominate the steppes, and the Manchu failed in Burma. Between 1775 and 1842, Britain was defeated in North America and intervened unsuccessfully in Argentina, Egypt, and Afghanistan.

I welcome a debate on how best to explain military change, not least because my work tends to emphasize continuities. Models that assume some mechanistic search for efficiency and a maximization of force do violence to the complex process by which interests in new methods interacted with powerful elements of continuity. For example, the varied response to firearms is best understood not in terms of military progress or administrative sophistication or cultural superiority but rather as a response to the different tasks and possibilities facing the armies of the period, within a context in which it was far from clear which weaponry, force structure, tactics, or operational method were better. To stress variety is not a "cop out" but, rather, a reminder of the flaws of schematic interpretations and an attempt to recreate the uncertainty and confusion within which choices and changes occur.

Thinking about Military Revolution

Dennis Showalter

From the relatively humble beginnings of a lecture delivered in what was a secondary British university and a pamphlet published in a city then hardly noted as an intellectual center, the concept of military revolution has metastasized. It has metastasized semantically, subdividing into the "military technological revolution," which focuses on weapons systems; the "revolution in military affairs," involving related but not comprehensive bodies of innovation in warmaking; and the "military revolution" *pur*, a comprehensive upheaval "uncontrollable, unpredictable, and unforeseeable" that brings systemic changes not merely to armed forces but to states and societies. Military revolution has metastasized historically. From its original location in the late sixteenth and early seventeenth centuries, it has been extended backwards into the Middle Ages and forwards to the contemporary era with stopovers in the mid-nineteenth and early twentieth centuries. Military revolution has metastasized geographically. Its initial location in northern Europe, specifically the Netherlands and Sweden, has expanded first to most of the continent including the British Isles, then to Asia, Africa, and the Ottoman Empire. And finally, military revolution has metastasized conceptually. Its original paradigm of an episodic process with relatively clear beginnings and ends is being challenged by an alternate concept of development over centuries, with particular actions and reactions less significant than the underlying pattern of steady modernization. In the more extreme version of this thesis, military *revolution* becomes for practical purposes military *evolution* and invites incorporation into the Whig/Marxist approach of history as progress.

The *disputatio* between Jeremy Black and Geoffrey Parker presented here involves intellectual adversaries who invite preliminary categorizing in the context of Isaiah Berlin's famous dichotomy. Black is a fox, a wide-ranging investigator who in the context of war studies takes the world for his province and challenges traditional wisdoms regarding "the West and the Rest." Parker is a hedgehog. No less wide-ranging intellectually, his scholarship and his reasoning alike remain solidly based in the Western experience of the sixteenth and seventeenth centuries. Black's argument is that military revolution, however it is defined and wherever it appears, depends ultimately on military organization. Organization is institutional, by its nature favoring the long term and the slow hand. Its totemic gas is nitrogen. Parker, on the other hand, makes his case for the centrality to military revolution of technology-based innovations and the research bases and mentalities underpinning them. These innovations energize. They inspire "aha" moments. By their nature they are episodic, involving the kind of paradigm shifts discussed by Thomas Kuhn. They have the impact of oxygen.

Oxygen: the musket and the countermarch can both be more or less pinpointed in time. Nitrogen: the regiments that brought these innovations into battle effectively defy such precise locating. Even the Spanish *tercio,* whose history has been so well delineated by Parker himself, was in good part a product of evolution, in the sense of dozens of modifications introduced in a basic structure over a *longue durée.* And thereby, perhaps, a way emerges not to reconcile the respective arguments presented here but to synergize them—or perhaps, in Hegelian terms, present them in dialectical rather than confrontational contexts.

On the one hand, military organizations regard technical innovation, the entering edge of military revolution, instrumentally. Organizations can—and do—persist independently of material changes, sometimes for centuries. Limited space constrains me to offer a simplistic example, albeit one culturally appropriate for our two principal contributors: Britain's Household Cavalry traces an unbroken institutional history from the mid-seventeenth century. Its primary technologies, however, have ranged from a half dozen and more types of sword, through Lee-Enfield rifles and (in a brief World War I avatar as part of the Guards Machine–Gun Regiment) Vickers heavy machine guns, to wheeled scout and armored cars, to tracked reconnaissance vehicles. And through it all they have remained the Guards.

From Sweden to India, other armies can show similar long-running lineages. That stability in turn makes military organizations the counterpoint to military revolutions. Organizations are regularly perceived as antagonists by reforming individuals like the current U.S. secretary of defense, by agencies, such as, the U.S. Office of Net Assessment, and by scholars like Shelford Bidwell and Dominick Graham in their classic *Fire-Power.* Yet revolutions, military and otherwise, are not automatic processes. Without organization, innovation atrophies. The countermarch, for example, and all of its successive ramifications might be mastered individually but could only be employed collectively—not even by groups of trained individuals but by stable organizations, institutions whose members were positively committed to a common enterprise: the regiment. That did not mean literally every regiment in every army had to be a permanent fixture. Rather, the concept of permanence as an ideal state needed to replace the entrepreneurial mentality dominant in an earlier military era. And military permanence in turn was a function of stable state organization and the social stability it in turn fostered.

The reverse side of that coin is the fate of organizations, from regiments to states, failing to keep pace with the innovations of war, the military technical revolutions, and the concepts supporting and extending them. Particularly in the modern West, characterized if not defined by extensive civil-military interaction and widespread transfer of ideas and research, those members of an alliance that reduce their military effectiveness in favor of, let us say, domestic social programs tend to become clients. To pick up another of Parker's points, had the United States during World War II restricted, for the sake of alliance compatibility, developing its technological capacities vis-à-vis Britain, the principal daylight escort fighter of 1944 might well have been some variant of Spitfire. D-Day would have been undertaken with an armored force depending on Cromwells, Grants, and perhaps a few Crusaders or Covenanters faute de mieux. To go back a step farther, had Britain scaled its military preparation to France in 1939–40, the language of this dialogue might well be German.

Parker's related point about "singleton techniques" becoming isolated in cultures lacking a broad pattern of flexibility applies on the organizational as well as the technological side. Systems with unstable or incomplete organizations are also prone to "one-off" institutional changes that eventually atrophy for lack of reinforcement and absence of context. This holds for the West as well as the Rest. Nazi Germany's capacity to introduce even a revolution in military affairs was severely limited by its failure—in good part a deliberate decision on Hitler's part—comprehensively to dismantle or emasculate German secondary institutions. Soviet Russia was admirably adapted to the mass, low-tech, industrial form of war that culminated from 1941 to 1945. But it was unable to meet the specific military challenges of the technotronic era, much less the general ones posed by an emerging information/electronic age. The result was implosion: collapse not from imperial but internal overstretch.

Even military revolutions—to say nothing of military technological revolutions and revolutions in military affairs—are to a significant degree susceptible to organizational control. It might even be argued that such control is necessary in their more specifically *military* aspects. The armies of the French Republic were manifestations of a military revolution in an early stage. But in their revolutionary format, they were regularly given all they could handle and more, from the Low Countries to Italy, by their unreformed and reactionary opponents. Only as the challenges and opportunities of the 1790s led to the organizing of the new forces, in durable institutions with strong roots in the past (the demibrigades of the *amalgame* come easiest to mind) did Napoleon's breakthroughs become possible.

To add examples would be to strain the framework of a general discussion. It seems worthwhile, however, to approach the subject of military revolution and its increasingly complex ramifications from a synthetic perspective, seeking to cross intellectual fault lines wherever possible if only for the sake of clearing a half-century's intellectual underbrush.

On the Once and Future RMA

Jeffrey Clarke

G iven Geoffrey Parker's specialization, it is not surprising that his presentation begins to lose a certain fidelity as it transitions into the twentieth century and especially into the contemporary decade.[1] But to his credit, Parker has discovered that the term *revolution in military affairs*—widely acronymed RMA—has great resonance with current defense decision makers and thinkers, including many of the world's principal heads of state and their closest advisers. The literature on the subject is extremely rich and, although generally not written by historians, makes extensive use of historical analogies for both scholarly and partisan purposes. Although few of today's RMA exponents would admit to any similarities with Parker's early modern European models, useful parallels certainly exist.

First, some comments on the current RMA debate—the term refers to contemporary advances in electronic communications that link battlefield sensors ("target-acquisition devices," such as satellites, drones, radar, and the like) with semiautomated weapons, allowing for an almost immediate tactical response and greatly accelerating the tempo of war. As usual, current military jargon reflects many of the associated concepts: "network-centric warfare" (the need to bypass traditional military chains of command that slow down this exchange), "distributed combat systems" (the transition from "platform-centric" combat machines to a wide variety of electronically linked "smart" devices such as precision-guided munitions, or PGMs), and "effects-based operations" (the ability to "engage targets" in the most economical fashion). (At this point I must apologize and ask the readers' indulgence for the euphemisms, acronyms, and plain bureaucratic jargon endemic to the subject matter.) In sum wasteful artillery barrages and air bombardments will be things of the past, and tanks and jet "fighters" will no longer fight—their

From *Historically Speaking* 4 (April 2003)

remote sensors and weapons will. Above all, "information dominance," the ability constantly to locate enemy forces on and off the battlefield and hide one's own, will be critical. At the macro level, Alvin Toffler and Heidi Toffler's grand vision of what they term the Third, or Information, Wave warfare (following a First, or Agrarian, Wave, beginning ten thousand years ago, and a Second, or Industrial, Wave, during the past three hundred years) provide popular context.[2]

No one, of course, claims that this Information Age RMA has yet occurred, only that its full-blown appearance is imminent and that certain elements—the televised Gulf War PGMs—have been evident for some time. One of the most prominent RMA champions, Admiral William Owens (former vice chairman of the Joint Chiefs of Staff and author of *Lifting the Fog of War*) recently argued that the revolution has suffered a partial setback in the United States since 1998, a "thermidorian reaction" caused partly by service parochialism and partly by the limited office terms of military and political leaders, which undermine policy continuity.[3] For Owens, the adoption of the term *transformation* in lieu of *revolution* to describe ongoing changes in the military establishment reflects an unsettling but, he hopes, temporary trend. In any case, he believes passage to true military revolution inevitable, even if it has to be driven primarily by advances in civilian communications technology. For others, however, the future is not so certain. The attacks on New York City's Twin Towers and the Pentagon seemed an effects-based PGM operation in reverse, while events such as the dispersal of nerve gas in a Tokyo subway, anthrax and sniper scares in the nation's capital, and the increasing number of terrorist bombings worldwide have raised the specter of "asymmetrical warfare"—threats that avoid U.S. conventional military superiority and play to its weaknesses—all of which narrow definitions of RMA fail to address.

These headline developments have encouraged broader RMA vistas more amenable in certain ways to the ideas that Parker attributes to Jeremy Black. For example, military analyst Michael Mazarr's definition of RMA adds three additional factors to information technology: "synergy" (the perfection of multiservice and multinational military capabilities), "disengaged combat" ("casualty-adverse" methods that promote "force protection" in recognition of the changing social mores of the industrialized democracies), and "civilianization" (the blurring of military and nonmilitary communities such as found in "cyber-warfare").[4] Another defense guru, Jeffrey Cooper, takes an even broader stand, contrasting past RMAs, "such as [the] development of the Macedonian phalanx and the Roman legion . . . with the Napoleonic RMA (the 'nation in arms')" and those of the late-nineteenth and twentieth centuries involving breech-loading artillery, the machine gun, the blitzkrieg (the favorite historic RMA of contemporary thinkers), and U.S. Navy carrier aviation, amphibious assault, and long-range submarine operations in World War II to name a few—RMAs galore for everyone, even if slightly slanted toward purely technological models.[5]

More useful, perhaps, is Cooper's division of RMAs into three categories: those "impelled by purely military technology," those "emphasizing . . . organization and operational innovations," and those "driven by fundamental economic, political, and social changes" ("the classic example").[6] For David Jablonsky, of the Army War College, the third definition seems preferable, especially given the preponderance of unconventional missions assigned to the services today (such as, peacekeeping, disaster relief, counterinsurgency, drug interdiction, and the like). Jablonsky also gives more weight to Michael Roberts's (*The Military Revolution, 1560–1660*) emphasis on tactics, strategy, size of armies, and sociopolitical institutions to explain the early modern military revolution, devoting much of his current analysis to changes in today's "sociopolitical dimension."[7]

The U.S. Army's official historians have their own views on these matters. They favor a multicausal approach to history, while characterizing current military affairs as "transformational."[8] Service historians have made the case for transformation through a series of extensive information papers and historical briefings. While inevitably (and sometimes shamefully) oversimplifying the historical past for its high-profile "student" audience, these presentations have focused on three causative factors from six case studies, each derived from the service's recent past. The causative factors include "technological advance," "strategic circumstance," and "socioeconomic change." The case studies showcase the transition from (1) frontier army to army for empire, ca. 1900, then to (2) European expeditionary force, 1917–18, and back to (3) hemispheric defense, 1919–40, returning to (4) expeditionary force, worldwide, 1941–45, and back once again to (5) constabulary army, 1946–50, before morphing into (6) the army of the cold war, 1950–90. Depending on the audience (medical, signal, engineer, or departmental-level officials, for example), subsidiary areas are included as appropriate.

For the first transition, the major impetus came from the end of the frontier and the overseas commitments occasioned by the war with Spain, with progressivism reflected in [then–secretary of state] Elihu Root's reform of the War Department and the attention paid to the army's medical and public health missions. For the second, it was "strategic circumstance" along with the industrialized war economy rather than new weapons that shaped the transformation of the U.S. Army into a leading conventional force during

World War I, and for the third, social and political factors after that war that conditioned its interwar nature—an institution responsible primarily for mobilization planning with its technology focused on coastal artillery systems that would ultimately prove superfluous. For a medical sidebar, the European war led to the massive acceleration of medical specialties, while the period that followed saw the growth of a civilian medical-research community that had increasing influence over its military counterpart.

The 1917 process repeated itself during World War II when global demands (again, "strategic circumstance") and American industry dictated the form that the army would take—although U.S. ground forces never really matched the military technology of their deadliest foe. In fact, only in the brief, postwar constabulary period did technology condition the size, organization, and expected mission of the army when the appearance of nuclear weapons seemed to make both mobilization and conventional combat obsolete. For the final case, the Korean War and the state of almost permanent mobilization that followed (the peacetime draft) ended these reveries, with technical advances being limited to relatively minor improvements in existing systems. Although helicopters allowed military physicians to centralize and expand their capabilities farther behind the battlefield, more significant was the gradual centralization of military policy in the largely civilian Department of Defense through its growing control over budgets and acquisition. In addition, changing social mores had great impact on the army's gender and ethnic composition, as well as on its ethical conduct in war and peace as the century moved to a close.

Much to the disappointment of our receptive audience, we service historians offered no detailed recipes for the future. Even policy wonks remind us that war is a chaotic enterprise, difficult to predict and dependent on such elements as the irrational actions of opponents, a variety of changing background conditions, and chance.[9] In sum, if the past is at all instructive, our brief historical sojourn shows that factors other than technology are also significant forces for change. Despite the seeming ease with which technological progress can be identified and even controlled, political, social, and economic elements have been more decisive. Certainly for the current U.S. Army, it was the end of the cold war and the difficulty of rapidly displacing heavy forces to places like Kuwait, Haiti, and Kosovo that underlined the need for drastic change, circumstances that are easily recalled by today's military leaders.[10]

Other analogous presentations have focused on the importance of military education and the false promises of "silver bullet" technology. From the claims of military prophets like Giulio Douhet and J. F. C. Fuller to those of the current crop of information-dominance advocates, all seem to rise phoenix-like from the ashes of every war. Few, however, have proved accurate. Playing the devil's advocate, army historians have even argued that the development of air-delivered PGMs has been driven more by the increasing effectiveness of air defenses (and the Vietnam-era specter of pilot hostages) rather than by any vision of network-centric, effects-based warfare. If anything, our historical analyses have highlighted the value of synergy at the tactical, or combat, level, arguing for organizations and training regimes that stress inter-arms jointness, which complicate an adversary's problems, rather than single solutions, which simplify them. Thus for today's army, such works as Colonel Douglas Macgregor's *Breaking the Phalanx: A New Design for Landpower in the Twentieth Century,* advocating major organization changes, make more sense than those of authors advocating primarily technical solutions to the challenges of future combat.[11]

For Parker's essay, then, I offer some notes of caution on the importance of technology or his prescriptions for the contemporary world. Regarding the numerical superiority of non-Western nations, the Gulf War may not be the best example, and in any case the industrialized democracies have shown themselves capable of marshaling forces overseas when they have chosen to do so. However, his implication that current world demographics (such as, the graying of the West) may shape future conflict is sound. I also agree with his assertion that Western technology has reflected Theodore Ropp's old "felt need" model (at least I think that is what Parker meant by "path-dependent, sequential"), but the underlying drivers seem to be socioeconomic and political. Although World War I technologies were generally adapted from the commercial sector (wireless, internal-combustion engine, chemicals), the reverse was true during World War II (radar, television, jet engines, nuclear energy, and the like), with the migration going both ways in today's much more technologically conscious world. But, to question one of Parker's closing points, globalism, outsourcing, and current communications technology have accelerated the spread of advanced military technology—a major problem facing the United States today—undermining our ability to hide and compartmentalize it. And does victory always follow from superior military technology and democratic civilian leadership as Parker asserts? Several European nations might disagree, while our own experiences in Southeast Asia are not encouraging. One could also question whether we should rein in our technological advances to accommodate allies whose defense budgets are proportionally so much smaller than our own or whether the anti-intellectualism of the American military establishment is not part of a larger national ethos.[12]

Regarding the former, if electronic digitization can be combined with new power sources and energy-directed weapons (sending air platforms into the trash bin), then some sort of revolution might truly take place. But regardless of these somewhat epilogical points, our readers can rejoice a bit today. For unlike Lipsius, the pace of the modern world will soon give them a ringside seat on those revolutionary transformations that do take place over the next decade. Thus, in the end, they can surely measure and weigh them personally, making their own informed judgments before the future once again transforms itself into the delightfully troublesome past.

NOTES

1. The views expressed in this essay are those of the author and do not necessarily reflect the official policy of the Department of the Army, the Department of Defense, or the U.S. government.

2. Alvin Toffler and Heidi Toffler, *War and Anti-War Survival at the Dawn of the Twenty-First Century* (Boston: Little, Brown, 1993).

3. William Owens, "The Once and Future Revolution in Military Affairs," *Joint Forces Quarterly* 31 (2002): 55–61.

4. Michael Mazarr, *The Revolution in Military Affairs: A Framework for Defense Planning* (Carlisle, Penn.: U.S. Army War College Monograph, 1994), 8–27.

5. Jeffrey Cooper, *Another View of the Revolution in Military Affairs* (Carlisle, Penn.: U.S. Army War College Monograph, 1994), 13–14.

6. Ibid., 20–21.

7. David Jablonsky, *The Owl of Minerva Flies at Twilight: Doctrinal Change and Continuity and the Revolution in Military Affairs* (Carlisle, Penn.: U.S. Army War College Monograph, 1994), 16–18, and chapter 4 (the best of the three Strategic Studies Institute products cited above).

8. The service's history office, the Center of Military History (CMH), is a small agency located at Fort McNair in the District of Columbia and consists of about one hundred historians and related professionals—curators, editors, archivists, graphic and topographic artists, and so forth. Outside professional oversight is provided by a primarily academic historical advisory committee, currently chaired by Gerhard Weinberg, that also has included many prominent members of the American military-history community in its fifty-plus years of existence. Best known perhaps for its publications (offered for public sale by the Government Printing Office and sent to over one thousand Federal Depository Libraries) and for its museums (over one hundred with almost one million annual visitors), the center also provides direct support to army political and military leaders on a wide variety of subjects from the esoteric to the mundane.

9. Mazarr, *Revolution in Military Affairs*, 7.

10. For an insightful treatment, see Peter Boyer, "A Different War: Is the Army Becoming Irrelevant?" *New Yorker*, July 1, 2002: 54–67.

11. For the current information on actual transformation, including OSD and service progress reports, visit the Web sites at www.eisenhowerseries.com, www.ifpaflet cherconference.com, and www.can.org/newsevents/conferences, which should eventually have transcripts and videotapes of recent "strategic" conferences sponsored by various defense-related organizations.

12. For a thoughtful discussion, see Colonel Lloyd Matthews, "The Uniformed Intellectual and His Place in American Arms, Part 1: Anti-Intellectualism in the Army Yesterday and Today," *Army* (July 2002): 17–25.

Random Thoughts of a Hedgehog

Geoffrey Parker

So Dennis Showalter has finally discovered my secret: "Parker is a hedge-hog!" I first came across Michael Roberts's inaugural lecture "The Military Revolution, 1560–1660" as an undergraduate in 1964, and the last chapter of my doctoral dissertation in 1968 (with Roberts as an examiner) sought to explain why his "model" did not seem to fit the Spanish Army of Flanders. That chapter eventually appeared as an article in 1976. I began work on *The Military Revolution* in 1982 and published it six years later.[1] This is indeed a hedgehog's pace compared with Jeremy Black, who first published on the subject in 1991 but refers the persevering reader to no less than twelve of his books—covering several thousand pages—since then. Small wonder that, looking back, Black finds that his "ideas have developed over the years," and he "can spot differences in emphasis in [his] work." Nevertheless, as he says, his oeuvre has "remained consistent in emphasizing diversity within both the West and the Rest," and every book bristles with examples and counterexamples from around the world.

This does not always aid historical clarity. Sir Isaiah Berlin's celebrated essay "The Hedgehog and the Fox," cited by Showalter, discussed the lapidary views about history in Leo Tolstoy's epilogue to *War and Peace.* Having portrayed as the backdrop to his novel the enormous upheavals that engulfed Europe in the early nineteenth century, which his contemporaries ascribed to the "genius" (sometimes "evil genius") of Napoleon Bonaparte, Tolstoy (who did not himself use the "fox" or "hedgehog" metaphors) questioned whether Napoleon had in fact shaped those upheavals and concluded that he did not: "A contemporary event seems to us indubitably the doing of all the men we know of concerned in it; but in the case of a more remote event we have had

From *Historically Speaking* 4 (April 2003); © Geoffrey Parker, 2003. Reproduced by permission of Greene & Heaton Ltd.

time to observe its inevitable consequences, which prevent our conceiving of anything else as possible. And the farther back we go in our investigation of events the less arbitrary do they appear." So Tolstoy tried to portray Napoleon as one man among many wrestling with a variety of forces and influences over which he had little control and whose outcome he could not predict.[2]

History, as Tolstoy recognized, often works in a nonlinear fashion. The simplest and most compelling illustration of the logic of the process is the "Polya urn" thought experiment. Imagine a large vessel containing two small balls, one red and one blue. Players are supposed to remove one ball at random, and return it to the urn, accompanied by an additional ball of the same color. And they are supposed to repeat this procedure until the urn has been filled. If the Polya urn starts out with one red ball and one blue one, then the odds of picking either one start out as even; but once the first move is made, and a player picks a ball (say red) and returns it with a like ball, the odds shift. There are now two red balls and only one blue. On the next move, the odds of picking red are now 2–1, and if a red ball is indeed picked and returned with a mate, there will then be three red balls to one blue. The chances of picking a red ball have thus risen from 50 percent to 75 percent in just two moves, and if one keeps picking in accord with the prevailing chances, which increasingly favor red, the odds climb so swiftly that red balls will soon be dominant. It is then very easy to forget that at one time the odds of the urn becoming virtually completely red or virtually completely blue were even.[3]

The rise of the West was just such a nonlinear process. Jeremy Black's desire to "recreate the uncertainty and confusion within which choices and changes occur" is therefore commendable, but it can only take us so far in explaining how the West managed to acquire domination over 85 percent of the world's land and most of its oceans by 1914. After a certain point, the potential of "uncertainty and confusion" to halt or derail Western expansion dwindles. Thus although between 1775 and 1842 Britain "intervened unsuccessfully in Argentina, Egypt, and Afghanistan," these failures pale in significance beside the simultaneous acquisition of direct control over a numerous population and prodigious resources in India. Likewise, although there is indeed "a need to encourage research in a number of fields that have been relatively understudied, for example, the military history of Southeast Asia and the 'Horn' of Africa," and although it would doubtless illuminate why those areas managed to resist Western conquest for so long, nevertheless the survival of a few such blue balls in the Polya urn neither alters nor explains the fact that by 1914 almost all the rest were red.

Nonlinear progressions occur frequently in military history. To take the example discussed above, until the 1590s many different theories existed concerning the effective use of muskets in the field; afterwards there was only one. This affected far more than tactics on the battlefield, because victory normally went to those units that had trained longest and best. Therefore, as one of Louis XIV's generals observed a century later, "One must always maintain in peacetime more infantry than cavalry, because it takes five or six years to create an [effective] infantry regiment and it only takes one year to create a good cavalry regiment."

So the *stippelckens* drawn by William Louis of Nassau in his letter of December 8, 1594, led to changes that transformed not only the equipment and tactics of infantry throughout the Western world but also their training and cost, with important implications for state formation as well as for the military balance between the West and the Rest. Time and again, infantry volley fire enabled Western troops to defeat far larger numbers of non-Western adversaries. It formed, in the words of the Duke of Wellington, "the foundation of the British strength in Asia, and of that opinion by which it is generally supposed that the British Empire has been gained and upheld. These qualities show in what manner nations consisting of millions are governed by thirty thousand strangers."[4]

The problem facing military planners today is to spot nonlinear trends before they gather momentum—to identify the "two moves" when the odds of picking a red ball from the Polya urn change from 1–1 to 3–1. Unfortunately for them, such tipping points (whether we call them military revolutions or revolutions in military affairs) often happen with little warning. If Wellington, the victor over Napoleon at Waterloo in 1815, had somehow returned as a spectator to the battles fought over the same terrain in the opening campaigns of World War I, one century later, he would have understood much of what was happening (although no doubt feeling insanely jealous of the improved speed and accuracy of small-arms fire.) However, had a commander from 1914 returned to the war four years later, he would have been totally mystified by the tanks, aircraft, and stormtroopers. Today the pace of change in military affairs has become even faster. As Jeffrey Clarke correctly notes, "Globalism, outsourcing, and current communications technology have accelerated the spread of advanced military technology" even more, "undermining our ability to hide and compartmentalize it." That is why it is so important for military planners to monitor all military developments, to spot the moment when the odds shift abruptly from 1–1 to 3–1, and to mobilize swiftly all the relevant research available to exploit their insight.

This, however, requires strategists to look outside their national traditions and experience. It is easier said than done—as Clarke's article, perhaps unconsciously, reveals. Thus his statement that the September 11 attacks and "the increasing number of terrorist bombings worldwide have *raised* the specter of 'asymmetrical warfare'" will exasperate those who lived in (say) Great Britain in the late twentieth century, where the security forces battled "asymmetrical warfare" for three decades with one hand tied behind their back because of foreign financial support for IRA terrorists—most of it from the United States! Repeated appeals from the British ministers to their U.S. counterparts to intervene proved vain. Likewise, as late as June 2001, when President Bush visited Spain and Prime Minister Aznar pleaded for support in his "war against terrorism" (in his case, against ETA, generously assisted from France), Bush remained indifferent and uninterested. Only September 11 led the United States to take elementary steps such as freezing the assets of organizations suspected of supporting terrorism elsewhere (just as those attacks forced the United States to adopt measures long standard abroad, such as screening all baggage at airports or banning knives and box cutters in carry-on luggage aboard domestic flights). Similarly Clarke's disparagement of the proposition that the United States "should rein in our technological advances to accommodate allies whose defense budgets are so proportionally smaller than our own" in order to retain allies capable of fighting by its side reveals a disappointingly narrow concept of "defense." The United States currently spends $400 billion a year to secure global peace and security, and yet its citizens face repeated "orange" or "red" alerts because even this prodigious expenditure cannot eliminate "low-tech/high-concept" threats like September 11. Perhaps some of the money saved from the defense budget by reining "in our technological advances to accommodate allies" could be used instead to address the widespread impoverishment and despair that breeds the frustration and instability on which terror thrives. The federal government recognized the need to do this between 1948 and 1951, when President Truman and General Marshall allocated billions of dollars to assist the recovery of the shattered economies of free Europe, while still financing a huge military panoply. But those days are gone. Now, whereas the ratio of defense spending to foreign aid in Denmark is 1.6 to 1 and in Britain 6 to 1, in the United States it is 35 to 1. Without a return to the enlightened vision of the Marshall Plan, even if they have a "ringside seat on those revolutionary transformations [in the art of war] that do take place over the next decade," it seems to me unlikely that "our readers can rejoice a bit." But, then, what would a hedgehog know about rejoicing?

NOTES

1. Readers interested in the "humble begins" of Roberts's "lecture delivered in what was a secondary British university" will find material in Geoffrey Parker,

"Michael Roberts 1908–1996," *Proceedings of the British Academy* 115 (Biographical Memoirs of Fellows, I): 333–54.

2. L. N. Tolstoy, *War and Peace,* trans. Rosemary Edmonds, 2 vols. (New York: Penguin, 1957), 2: 1433; Isaiah Berlin, *The Hedgehog and the Fox: An Essay on Tolstoy's View of History* (New York: Simon and Schuster, 1953).

3. See Philip Tetlock and Geoffrey Parker, "Conclusion: Counterfactual History: Its Advocates, Its Critics, And Its Uses," in *Unmaking the West: "What-If?" Scenarios That Rewrite World History,* ed. Philip Tetlock, Ned Lebow, and Geoffrey Parker (Ann Arbor: University of Michigan Press, 2006).

4. Jean Bérenger, *Turenne* (Paris: Fayard, 1987), 383–84, quoting the memoirs of the marquis of Chamlay, personal military adviser to Louis XIV; D. George Boyce, "From Assaye to the *Assaye:* Reflections on British Government, Force, and Moral Authority in India," *Journal of Military History* 63 (1999): 647–48, quoting Wellington in 1805.

War Made New

An Interview with Max Boot

M ax Boot is senior fellow for national security studies at the Council
on Foreign Relations. His *War Made New: Technology, Warfare, and
the Course of History, 1500 to Today* (2006) examines how technological
revolutions have transformed warfare and the global balance of power.
Boot spoke to *Historically Speaking* editor Donald A. Yerxa on December 7,
2006.

DONALD A. YERXA: What is your basic argument in *War Made New?*
MAX BOOT: What I do in *War Made New* is to look at what military
thinkers call revolutions in military affairs—major upheavals that occur when
you have new technology combining with new doctrine, training, and organization to transform the face of battle as well as the international system. I
argue that there have been four such major transformations—although you
can certainly dispute the categorization—over the course of the last five hundred years: the Gunpowder Revolution beginning around 1500; the First
Industrial Revolution, whose impact on warfare began to be felt about 1850
or so; the Second Industrial Revolution centered on the technologies of the
internal-combustion engine, the airplane, and radio, whose full impact was
felt in World War II; and the Information Revolution driven by advances in
microchip technology since the 1960s. I argue that in order to understand the
world as it came to be, you have to understand these revolutions in military
affairs. Obviously, there have been many historians who have written about
each of these individual revolutions and the upheavals that resulted from
them. But what I try to do is to put this history together in a sweeping and
comprehensive way. I also bring the story up to the present day and to the
near future in looking at the impact of the Information Revolution as it is

playing out now and other potential revolutions on the horizon that are likely to make their effects felt in years to come.

YERXA: Do these revolutions in military affairs have a common genesis?

BOOT: Generally, most of these revolutions are sparked by advances in a cluster of technologies that occur over a fairly concentrated period of time, although it is getting more concentrated now than it was hundreds of years ago. Very often these inventions will come out of left field. Whether it's gunpowder, three-masted sailing ships, steam engines, telegraphs, airplanes, radio, automobiles, microchips, most inventions are not invented for military purposes at all. That's often the last thing on the inventor's mind. But, nevertheless, they are sooner or later harnessed—often sooner—for military purposes and begin to transform not only society but also what happens on the battlefield. The key test of success or failure in these revolutions in military affairs is who can best harness these inventions and change organizational structures, military doctrine, leadership, etc., in order to take advantage of what these new technologies allow.

YERXA: Clearly, then, revolutions in military affairs involve much more than technology by itself.

BOOT: Absolutely. I stress that in the book. Although revolutions in military affairs are centered on technology, this is not just a story about machines per se. It's really a story of how people adapted or failed to adapt to technology.

YERXA: And given the pace of technological innovation, we should expect that the intervals between the revolutions in military affairs will become shorter.

BOOT: That has been the experience over the last five hundred years. It took at least a couple hundred years for the Gunpowder Revolution to come to fruition; it took a long time for inventions to travel and for their full impact to be felt in the early modern period. The Industrial Revolution was a little faster, but arguably it still took as much as fifty to one hundred years for the impact of industrial technology to transform what happened on the battlefield. With the Second Industrial Revolution it was only a matter of a few decades. And the same is true of the Information Revolution. Most of the fundamental breakthroughs in microelectronics and other computer technologies date back from the late 1960s and early 1970s, and they have already had a huge impact on warfare over the course of the last ten or fifteen years. With technology the impact is cumulative, and the pace of scientific and technological progress is speeding up now. Even as the Information Revolution is still working its way through the system, we are witnessing huge developments already that may well transform warfare in the next few years in areas like robotics, nanotechnology, biological warfare, space war, cyber war, and directed-energy weapons. It is hard to predict which of these will actually be transformative in their impact, but the technology certainly has the potential to be revolutionary. There is no question that the pace of change is accelerating, and as a result the dangers of being left behind are increasing.

YERXA: Would you agree with military thinkers who maintain that though the character of war changes greatly, the nature of war is unchanging?

BOOT: That is exactly right. I am not some techno-utopian who claims that new machines make everything completely different, and everything that anybody has ever thought can be thrown out. It is ridiculous to talk about ending the "fog of war," for example. We are always going to have confusion; this is a constant. The fundamental nature of warfare is never going to change. At some elemental level it is always going to be a question of imposing your will on the enemy. And at that very basic level, war hasn't changed since the days of the hoplite. But, as you say, the character of war changes dramatically. You may have all the courage and fortitude of a Greek hoplite, but that's not going to do a heck of a lot of good facing an enemy with the modern machinery of war. So you had better adapt. In this kind of discussion, people tend to go to extremes. On the one hand, you have people who scoff at the notion that there is anything new under the sun and contend that warfare hasn't changed since the caveman days. And, on the other hand, there are people who say that anything that anyone thought thirty years ago is outdated because we have this amazing technology. What I try to do in *War Made New* is to provide a balanced perspective by looking at what changes and what doesn't change.

YERXA: The basic question of continuity and change, of course, is at the heart of all historical inquiry. And military historians and analysts are debating the extent to which military history is evolutionary or revolutionary. Your book certainly speaks to this.

BOOT: Obviously, since I have organized the book around revolutions, I am making the case that military history is not just a matter of small-scale innovations that accumulate over time. There are instances where you have a bunch of new technologies, military doctrines, and ways of fighting that completely transform the face of battle. I realize this is a controversial position, since nowadays there are historians who deny that the Renaissance or the Scientific Revolution existed. You can always have these arguments over whether you should categorize the past in terms of evolution as opposed to revolution. But I maintain that there are dramatic breaks with the past. On the specific matter of the current debates among military thinkers, I am a little skeptical of those who advance so-called fourth-generation theory—that is, those who argue that large-scale warfare between states is being eclipsed by unconventional, asymmetrical netwar. I do not think there has been a break-through in guerrilla or terrorist tactics that negates what conventional nation-state militaries do. Guerrilla warfare and terrorism are as old as recorded history. What is new today is that technology gives far more destructive capacity to relatively small bands of people. A century ago guerrillas may have been forced to operate in one region or one country. They might have been armed with rusty rifles, spears, and swords. Today, even in the most backward country in the world, everyone has an AK47 or a rocket-propelled grenade, and we see the proliferation of new, destructive technologies like guided mis-siles and, potentially, weapons of mass destruction. The guerrilla groups have far greater freedom of action because they are able to utilize jumbo jets, the Internet, satellite television, cell phones—all these modern technologies—to extend their insurgency around the world. The terrorists we face today are really superterrorists. They are much more powerful than previous genera-tions of guerrillas and potentially more powerful than entire armies were a century ago.

YERXA: Why has the West seemed better suited to embrace innovation in military matters?

BOOT: Clearly there is something in Western culture that has been a spur to these kinds of developments, but it is very hard to figure out what that something is. I've looked at a lot of literature on the subject, including the works of William McNeill, David Landes, Victor Davis Hanson, Thomas Sowell, Paul Kennedy, even Arnold Toynbee and Oswald Spengler. None of them has really reached a definitive answer. So many of the theories that have been entertained in the past have been shown to be wrong—for instance, Max Weber's contention that Protestantism is responsible for prosperity. Now we see many non-Protestant, indeed non-Christian, countries prospering. So it is hard to say exactly what dynamic is operating. There is some combina-tion of rationalism, dynamism, free inquiry, and capitalism that emerged in the early modern period and has been a huge spur to the West economically, militarily, and culturally. Some of that advantage continues, but it is rapidly eroding. The West has been spreading its ideas, its educational system, sci-ence, and technology all around the world, and this cultural dynamism is no longer a Western monopoly.

YERXA: You provide a number of battle narratives, ranging from the Span-ish Armada to the bombing of Tokyo, to support your analytical argument. What were some of the most unexpected things you learned as you researched these battles?

BOOT: One of the most surprising findings was how often the poorer, weaker power defeated the larger, richer power. In our society there is a kind of default assumption of economic determinism—that if you're big, rich, and powerful that automatically translates to success on the battlefield. It's just not so. In fact in many of the battles about which I wrote David defeated Goliath, starting with the Spanish Armada in 1588. England was much poorer and smaller than Spain, yet the English navy was much more adept at the new style of gunpowder warfare at sea than the Spanish navy was. As a result the Spanish Armada failed in its mission. There were so many other examples of this. In the battle of Tsushima Strait in 1905, Japan on paper was much smaller and weaker than Russia. Yet the Japanese proved to be much more adept at the new style of naval warfare, utilizing steel battleships firing high-explosive shells. And, more recently, the United States hasn't faired too well against adversaries in Vietnam and Iraq, notwithstanding that the resources we can bring to bear are vastly greater than those of our enemies. What this really shows to me is the central importance of skill at waging war. This is not a revolutionary insight on my part, but there has been a tendency to overlook this, especially in the academy. There is so little study of military history in universities today. There is an implicit assumption that what happens on the battlefield is irrelevant. All you have to do is look at the larger political, economic, and culture issues, and that tells you all you need to know. I don't think that is the case at all. Often the outcomes on battlefields have been very surprising to outside observers at the time and have had tremendously sweeping repercussions. Another great example is the battle of Königgrätz in 1866 where almost nobody predicted that the tiny Prussian state would beat the mighty Austrian Empire. People like Friedrich Engels were writing in the *Times of London* very confidently of how Prussia was going to be crushed. That didn't happen, of course, and because it didn't, you saw the rise the Prussian-dominated, militaristic German state. That wouldn't have happened if the Habsburg army had performed a little bit better on the battlefield of Königgrätz in July 1866. That is just one example of how the outcomes of these battles have really changed history. And it hasn't pivoted so much on underlying resources but on how you utilize these resources and what kind of training, leadership, and organization you have to fight. In twenty-first-century America that is an underappreciated factor in world history.

YERXA: I'd like to pursue the question of the health of military history in the academy. There has been a debate in recent years over whether military history, particularly traditional operational history, is in decline in the academy.

Clearly, you believe that academic historians tend to discount the importance of military history. Why do you think this is so?

BOOT: There is a definite bias against military history in today's academy. The problem may well be a function of the generation of faculty that we have teaching today. The previous generation had a much better appreciation for military history because so many were veterans of World War II. They had fought in a major war and understood the importance of military events, whereas so many of those on history faculties today were demonstrating against war in the 1960s or have been taught by those who did. I think their view is that studying war is akin to an endorsement of war. I find this to be a very strange notion. It is as if oncologists endorse cancer by studying it. There is also the other assumption that war just isn't important: the study of economic or cultural history reveals the underlying trends that have really driven history. It's the Braudelian-*Annales* school view that since wars are like the froth on the waves of history, why not pay attention to the more important currents that lie beneath? I'm not denying the importance of studying underlying forces, but I want to stress that it is very hard to understand the world as it exists without also understanding how wars were fought, how outcomes were determined, and—unfashionable as it is to say—the role of great captains in reshaping the battlefield and redrawing the map of the world. This last point suggests another prejudice: to study war, especially at the operational level, you have to understand the view from above, decisions made by generals and statesmen. These people are decidedly out of fashion at the moment because they tend to be "dead, white males." Now we want history from below, and we need to study history from that perspective. But there ought to be room for both kinds of history. Unfortunately, the desire to be revisionist and to come up with new approaches to the study of history has squeezed out some of the older approaches.

YERXA: How should the American military respond to the new realities of the twenty-first century? Does it need significant restructuring to meet threats from the militaries of hostile states as well as from terrorists and those who opt for unconventional or asymmetrical warfare?

BOOT: We need to restructure the military. There is a tendency to focus too much on the technological dimension of war and to think that there is a technological solution to every problem. This is a very American mindset. But one of the key themes in my book is that in order to harness the potential of a revolution in military affairs, you have to change not only your technology but also your organization. Right now, the U.S. leads the world in military technology, but we are not so good at harnessing it. We have all these smart bombs, which have their use, but we really need smart people to understand foreign cultures, foreign languages, counterinsurgency, state-building. We need people who understand our enemies, who can foil their plots, who can compete effectively for hearts and minds in the Muslim world. We don't have enough of those skill sets. And as long as that is the case, all of our aircraft carriers, cruise missiles, and all the rest of it is really not going to do us much good. It's not doing us much good in places like Afghanistan and Iraq today. We also need these skill sets in the State Department, CIA, USAID, so many parts of the government. And to create those skill sets we need to think about how to change training, recruitment, promotion criteria, and incentives. For example, in the military every officer changes jobs every two or three years. That makes it very hard to develop long-term expertise. The military values combat leaders much more than those who have knowledge of foreign cultures. As a result we have a surplus of tremendous combat leaders, but we don't have enough people who understand tribal relations in al-Anbar Province or what's going on in Kazakhstan. We've made some technological breakthroughs; now we need the organizational breakthroughs to go with them in order to face the enemies we are likely to face in the future.

YERXA: What do you wish the reader would take away from *War Made New?*

BOOT: I would hope the reader would find the book a good read and one that has a lot of relevance for the kinds of issues we have been talking about. I hope that the book places our current strategic dilemmas in broader historical perspective and that it will increase the reader's understanding of the defense and strategic challenges we now face that go beyond the headlines.

YERXA: How does *War Made New* relate to your previous book *Savage Wars of Peace?*

BOOT: Both books grew out of a desire to shed historical light on issues of present-day controversy. *Savage Wars of Peace* was my attempt to step back from some of the debates of the 1990s over low-intensity interventions in places like Bosnia, Kosovo, and Haiti and to look at similar interventions going back through two hundred years of American history. Likewise, in *War Made New* I try to shed historical light on the debate about defense transformation and the revolution in military affairs that has been raging in military circles since the Gulf War in 1991. So I'm trying to deal with current issues in a broad historical light.

PART 2

The Future of War

Been There! Done That!
Blood in the Crystal Ball

Colin S. Gray

A few years ago I was invited to write a book on "future warfare." My first reaction was to be skeptical. How could I write a book about nothing? There is no evading the fact that the future has yet to happen, a condition that necessarily leaves the ambitious author with no choice but to speculate. There is and can be no direct evidence. My sense of unreality was enhanced when I was requested to supply a list of illustrations and also of maps of future wars. Happily for my mental equilibrium, it did not take me too long to realize that we know a very great deal about future warfare, notwithstanding the contrary verdict that one might derive from the laws of physics that prohibit time travel. The result is my text *Another Bloody Century: Future Warfare.* The principal title reveals most of the plot.

It may be important for me to underline the fact that I am a social scientist, not a historian. By this admission I confess to being unafraid of big concepts, perhaps even to a fault. I am unhealthily attracted to theory and to examples that illustrate its workings. Moreover, I am perilously apt to seek and therefore find precedents and parallels across the ages (among my other sins against careful historical scholarship). In my defense I have to plead the professional bias of a social scientist and, scarcely less significant, thirty or so years of employment as a professional defense analyst.

Slowly, but inexorably, it dawned upon me that to write a book about "future warfare" was really only an attempt on a rather grand scale to do what I have been paid to do for most of my working life. All of my work for the government on nuclear targeting (which passes for strategy!), maritime strategy, space warfare, arms control, and the rest has been inalienably speculative. That feature of one's work is brought home pointedly when a student asks,

From *Historically Speaking* 7 (January/February 2006)

"What is the best book written on nuclear strategy?" The answer, perhaps an answer, is that I do not know, nor does anyone else, and "God willing and the creeks don't rise," we will never find out. But because strategy and strategic studies is a practical business, we social scientist-strategists, though comfortable with the uncertainties of an unknown future, are inclined to favor a short horizon of concern. Defense analysts, even if self-promoted to the grander-sounding class of strategic theorists, by and large serve official clients by addressing their problems. Strategic thought, original or, more frequently, highly derivative, is driven by the concerns of the day, the week, and just possibly the year.[1] This can be a *déformation professionelle.* With respect to our subject here, future warfare, social-science defense analysis, happily and profitably becomes a cottage service industry for the policy makers and military executives of today. It shares their assumptions and accepts the limitations of a relatively near-term focus.[2] All too often, social science is parked precariously between a past that it does not understand, let alone grasp how to use prudently, and a future that it approaches almost wholly through the prism of the issues and fashionable nostrums of today. What is missing, need I add, is historical perspective.

Historians, cursed as well as blessed by their knowledge (I won't claim understanding) of the course of events, are impaired as a consequence in their ability to empathize with historical figures. This is not a criticism: it is just the way things are. Historians are often all but overwhelmed by the rich contextuality of unique events. By contrast, social scientist–strategists habitually are in a like condition to actual historical agents: they must advise for an unknown and unknowable future. We social scientists, poverty stricken in our grasp of historical context and desperately short of perspective, badly need the services of a history profession willing and able to look beyond the length of a Macedonian sarissa (sixteen feet). *Another Bloody Century* attempts to make a case for the relevance of history: indeed, it does so to the fairly extreme point where it discounts the significance of much that is and will be novel in the twenty-first century.

It is my contention that our human future, especially with respect to war and warfare, will resemble our past. On two levels, at least, this claim is highly controversial. At the lower level, concerned with warfare, the conduct of war, I affront, or appear to do so, the views of those many defense experts who smell military revolution in the air. Current advocates of military "transformation" expect to achieve "a dramatic increase . . . in the combat potential and military effectiveness of armed forces."[3] How is this highly desirable outcome to be secured? The now standard definition, provided in 1994 by

Andrew F. Krepinevich, advises that "a military revolution . . . is what occurs when the application of new technologies into a significant number of military systems combines with innovative operational concepts and organizational adaptation in a way that fundamentally alters the character and conduct of conflict."[4]

In short we are asked to believe that the computer will fundamentally change the character of war. Well, I do not believe it. My problem is with Krepinevich's claim for fundamental change, not with the proposition that war changes its character. We have been there before. Modern weapons and industrial-age logistics did not produce the swift victory expected by many in 1914. Air power did not alter the fundamental character of warfare. And even the weaponization of atomic physics, though admittedly posing an exceptional challenge to the means-ends logic of strategy, has long been accommodated and, thank goodness, more or less effectively sidelined. There are no especially persuasive reasons why information technology (IT) should produce anything more significant than yet another major change in the way that some kinds of warfare are conducted by some belligerents. In other words, the twenty-first century will resemble the twentieth and the nineteenth, at least in the view of this theorist. It will witness major change in the character of some forms of warfare. But if we pause and ask the quintessential strategist's question, "So what?"—the answer is rather less exciting than the current official literature on military transformation might lead one to expect. I will hazard the opinion that the Information Revolution in military affairs will be of modest value, at most, in enhancing combat prowess and will be of close to no value at all in improving performance in war.

I have mentioned that my claim that our future will resemble our past is controversial on two levels. I have just dealt with the view that fundamental (a highly contestable adjective) change in warfare is underway and should be expected to produce transformative effects for its military beneficiaries. My response to that item of faith, resting, dare I say it, on this social scientist's reading of history, is a loud cry of caveat emptor! But there is a second, this time truly more fundamental level of analysis, wherein I have hunted down, poached perhaps, some fairly sacred beliefs and declared them to be vacuous. Where *Another Bloody Century* gives most offense, I am told, is in its resolute refusal to give any notable aid and comfort to the Whig interpretation of history. My view of history, let alone of strategic history, does not privilege the idea of progress, however defined. Although warfare is constantly changing, albeit at a variable rate among periods and societies, in their essentials war, warfare, and strategy do not change. I like to believe that that would-be master claim is inductively derived, not deductively chosen to suit my intellectual taste. Indeed, if my claim is not well founded, the value of strategic history as anything other than a playground for scholars must be called into question. I contend that in most important respects twenty-first-century warfare is not and will not be hard for us to understand. Why? Because we have two and a half millennia of highly variable access to past human experience of war. Moreover, that experience, for all the limitations of history, is the only source of evidence available to us.

It is sensible and necessary to highlight the inherent weaknesses of the history of historians as contrasted with history understood as the actual past. The distinguished military historian Antulio J. Echevarria, for example, pulls no punches when he warns that historians have no objective measure of the "extent [to which] the histories they write either capture or deviate from the past."[5] But I believe that he is overly pessimistic. As one of the last of the positivists, I hold to the romantic, certainly deeply unfashionable, opinion that in many cases we can aspire to achieve some approximation to historical truth. That is to say, we can reasonably hope to understand the past with our historical research and writing.

The intellectual basis of *Another Bloody Century* is my claim, following Clausewitz, naturally, that "all wars are things of the *same* nature."[6] If Clausewitz is correct in that unqualified claim and if I interpret him correctly (Echevarria and I have differed on this matter, but my opinion has not altered)[7], the nature of war is as constant as its character is subject to change. Moreover, that change can be dramatic and even apparently nonlinear, though most often it is cumulative and evolutionary. To quote the title to the editors' conclusions to by far the best study to date of military revolutions, it has to follow that "the future [is] behind us."[8]

I will risk testing the generosity of judgment of some readers at this point by offering two claims that many may regard as shocking. First, it does not really matter unduly if, to quote Napoleon (probably), history "is a fable agreed upon."[9] At least, I must hasten to add, it does not matter overmuch to defense professionals. We do not care about many of the details of warfare's changing character through two and a half millennia. What we care about is the unchanging nature of war. We need to know that warfare in all periods and of all kinds has had a "climate" comprising "danger, exertion, uncertainty, and chance."[10] Further, the variable character of the interplay among passion, chance, and reason is a permanent feature in the nature of war. In addition to war's unchanging climate, Clausewitz's nature of war includes the priceless compound concept of friction: the accumulation of unexpected difficulties that inevitably arise in war. This idea is as ubiquitous, as potent, and as enduring as it challenges militaries at all times to try to minimize its full consequences or even, hopelessly, to evade its authority altogether.[11]

In addition to the nature of war, which he insists is a duel for the proximate political purpose of imposing one's will on the enemy, Clausewitz also provides fundamental guidance on the nature of strategy. The essential point Clausewitz makes is that strategy "works" the same way, has the same meaning, and comprises exactly the same elements or dimensions—however they are clustered—regardless of time, place, technology, or issue. We have a general theory of strategy that is authoritative for the past, the present, and the future.

So, if I am right, or perhaps right enough, in believing that the great Prussian has armed us with a general theory of war and strategy that has universal and eternal validity in its basics, it should follow that we are tolerably well equipped intellectually to cope with whatever the twenty-first century may throw at us.

My second possibly shocking claim is that to the author of a book like *Another Bloody Century* or, indeed, any work on future war or warfare, the detailed character of warfare yet to come is both unknowable and not especially interesting or even important. We know that the human record in political, strategic, and scientific-technological prediction is extremely poor. That is not a historical fable. Of course, our politicians and soldiers are obliged to guess about the future of warfare as best they can, subject to fiscal constraint, the tolerance of public mood, the fashionable notions of the day, and the apparent lessons of recent experience. When a defense community, an inherently practical society, does its job of planning for national security, it is always at risk to the seduction of "presentism." If history is bunk, as a notable American once famously observed, then the world is ever made anew. We always have a clean strategic slate on which to write. That absurd assumption would be humorous were it not so often reflected in the reality of ahistorical, even antihistorical policy makers. In practice, though, not even the most benighted of Washington's believers in the authority of "rational choice" are truly ahistorical. Policy makers and soldiers who are severely challenged historically are just easy targets for the purveyors of shaky theories that have some historical decoration. The influence of history on policy-making is inescapable. The only choice is between better or worse history. To repeat, I am not overimpressed by Echevarria's valid point that there is no objective test for historical truth. That is simply the way it is. Since historical experience is literally the only source of evidence on strategic behavior available, unreliable though it must be, we are obliged to make the best of it.

Recently, it has been open season for books on the future of war.[12] To my mind, at least, the merit in these works tends to correlate negatively with their ventures into the airy realm of prediction. Such ventures naturally encourage advocacy. After all, if one claims to understand whither events are tending, one is all but obliged to recommend means and methods tailored to suit the new conditions. Past experience should be allowed to tell us that we prepare most capably for future warfare by being flexible and adaptable in our preparations. Surprise happens! This less than startling insight is as important as it is unhelpful to the defense planner. In common with friction, it is all but impossible to operationalize recognition of the salience of surprise. Clausewitz has a way of identifying great truths that require inspired judgment on the part of historical agents before their educational value can be employed to good effect. The concept of "the culminating point of victory" is another of his brilliant, if obvious, notions that is not particularly helpful to the politician or soldier who wonders just where that point is on the map.[13]

There is no good reason to believe that our extant general theory of war and strategy will prove inadequate in the face of the political, social, military, and environmental changes of the future. It is true that the vital contexts of war are always on the move. However, that movement matters not at all for the nature of war and strategy. What would matter, of course, would be change to war's political or social-cultural contexts on such a scale as to render war and strategy literally obsolete. Alas, that happy prospect is no more probable in the twenty-first century than it was in the twentieth, the nineteenth, or indeed any other. Sad to relate, perhaps, the true author of my ruling assumption that the crystal ball for our future shows a blood-stained vision is none other than Thucydides. What will future war be about? Why will humans fight with whatever technology provides? The answer is as clear as it is eternal: "fear, honor, and interest."[14] We see the future in our past. And the relevance of history? I will leave the last words in this essay to the greatest of modern strategic thinkers, Bernard Brodie: "The only empirical data we have about how people conduct war and behave under its stresses is our experience with it in the past, however much we have to make adjustments for subsequent changes in conditions."[15]

NOTES

1. In the sage words of Raymond Aron, "Strategic thought draws its inspiration each century, or rather at each moment of history, from the problems which events themselves pose" ("The Evolution of Modern Strategic Thought," in *Problems of Modern Strategy*, ed. Alastair Buchan [London: Chatto and Windus, 1970], 25).

2. Critics of strategic studies have complained about this incestuous relationship for at least forty years. It just is the case that official or industrial clients will not pay for what they deem to be unfriendly advice. Moreover, such advice will not be helpful. Policy and strategy making is the art of the possible. Advice of a truly radical kind, which reflects assumptions fundamentally at odds with current policy, generally will be utterly politically impracticable and therefore useless. I addressed these contentious matters many years ago in *Strategic Studies: A Critical Assessment* (Westport, Conn: Greenwood Press, 1982).

3. Andrew F. Krepinevich, "Cavalry to Computer: The Pattern of Military Revolutions," *National Interest* 34 (Fall 1994): 30.

4. Ibid.

5. Antulio J. Echevarria II, "The Trouble with History," *Parameters* 35 (Summer 2005): 80.

6. Carl von Clausewitz, *On War*, ed. and trans. Michael Howard and Peter Paret (Princeton: Princeton University Press, 1976), 606.

7. My exchange with Echevarria can be found in "Clausewitz and 'How Has War Changed?'" *Parameters* 35 (Summer 2005): 138–40.

8. Williamson Murray and MacGregor Knox, "Conclusion: The Future behind Us," in *The Dynamics of Military Revolution, 1300–2050*, ed. Knox and Murray (Cambridge: Cambridge University Press, 2001), 175–94.

9. Quoted in Echevarria, "Trouble with History," 81, albeit with a prudent "reportedly" added.

10. Clausewitz, *On War*, 104.

11. Barry D. Watts, *Clausewitzian Friction and Future War*, McNair Paper 68, rev. ed. (Washington, D.C.: National Defense University, 2004), is outstanding.

12. I am hardly in a position to criticize this phenomenon, given that I have added to it with *Another Bloody Century*. For some examples, see: Mark Cerasini, *The Future of War: The Face of Twenty-First-Century Warfare* (New York: Alpha, 2003); Christopher Coker, *The Future of War: The Re-Enchantment of War in the Twenty-First Century* (Oxford: Blackwell, 2004); Isabelle Duyvesteyn and Jan Angstrom, eds., *Rethinking the Nature of War* (Abingdon: Frank Cass, 2005); and Herfried Münkler, *The New Wars* (Cambridge: Polity, 2005).

13. Clausewitz, *On War*, 566.

14. Robert B. Strassler, ed., *The Landmark Thucydides: A Comprehensive Guide to "The Peloponnesian War,"* trans. Richard Crawley, rev. ed. (New York: Free Press, 1996), 43.

15. Bernard Brodie, "The Continuing Relevance of *On War*," in Clausewitz, 54.

Comment on Gray

Peter Paret

There is much that I agree with in Colin Gray's statement on the future of warfare and much that puzzles me in his exuberant declaration of independence from constraints that too often afflict historians. On a major point we see eye to eye. Technological development will always create new ways of fighting, but it has not changed the nonmilitary and military elements of intent and violence that together make up war. To the people who do the fighting, technological innovation necessarily looms large, and it is understandable if it colors their thoughts about every aspect of war. But a new level of destructiveness or more rapid and secure delivery systems cannot override such matters as the relationship among political goals, military aims, and the efforts to achieve them. Any attempt to predict how wars will be fought in the future must take account of this relationship, as well as of further technological development. It is easier to recommend ways in which the relationship may be strengthened than to predict how—or even that—it will be changed.

Since the 1960s this country has confronted opponents whose ideas on war and how to wage war have not always matched our expectations. Too often our political and military leaders have assumed that the other side would react as we might, a psychological and intellectual error difficult to avoid, perhaps especially so for a society with worldwide interests and commitments that nevertheless remains somewhat insular. Recent administrations have not always adopted realistic aims nor developed appropriate methods to achieve them. And neither in the 1960s nor today have they been good at explaining to the American public the broad lines of political and military policy in reasonably factual terms. But substantial public support may do more to win a war than a new weapons system. Perhaps not too much should be made of these deficiencies. In war the enemy is often misunderstood and

From *Historically Speaking* 7 (January/February 2006)

yet may be defeated, and even a malfunctioning political and military leadership may succeed—though presumably success would come at unnecessarily
high cost. But with whatever means future wars will be fought, the familiar
interaction of violence and politics between opponents (intensified by the
interaction in each belligerent of domestic and external politics with the use
of and exposure to violence) will again play itself out, whatever the technology employed.

With Gray I believe that Clausewitz helps us to think about war conceptually and comparatively. Clausewitz moves beyond the description and
analysis of the wars of his time to identify elements common to all wars. Two
of these are mentioned in Gray's appreciative discussion: "friction" and "the
culminating point of victory." Each exemplifies a different kind of common-
ality. "Friction" identifies the obvious fact that in something as complex as a
military force and in the even more complex interaction between two opposing forces, not everything will proceed as intended. Friction distinguishes
reality from plans or theory—less so if theory includes the concept of friction!
It forces us to think about imponderables rather than shrug them off as
unquantifiable and unanalyzable. The culminating point, in contrast, distinguishes a complex of hypotheses, pointing to possibilities that we are again
asked to think about: "even victory has a culminating point," beyond which
military and sometimes political advantage as well may shift from one side to
the other. Clausewitz places these and similar facts and hypotheses into a
wider framework of strategic decisions and political intent. His discussion is
focused on particulars, whether they relate to organization, tactics, strategy,
or policy, but they are analyzed as immediately or potentially linked.

It was through personal experience and study—the study of theory and
especially of history—that Clausewitz identified these elements and proposed
that they are common to war as such. He read widely in military theory from
Machiavelli to authors of his own day and borrowed, adapted, or rejected
much. But he read even more widely in the historical literature and himself
wrote a great many historical studies, mainly but by no means exclusively on
war. He understood that no historian could know everything or could be
totally objective, but he believed that much *could* be known and that even
imperfect objectivity was worth reaching for. Judging from his reactions to
the work of others, he appears to have felt that a historian's subjectivity and
limited knowledge could be largely rectified by well-informed, critical readers as long as they, in turn, tried to be evenhanded.

Since Clausewitz's extensive historical studies and writings were an essential part in the process by which he developed his ideas on war, it seems strange
that Gray posits such a deep division between theorists, especially theorists

who speculate about the future, and historians. But whether we like it or not, it is a given that historical interpretations are affected by the present and often by concern for the future. To generalize about war as it is today and may always have been is certainly not the same as predicting how war may be fought in the future. Still, generalizations about the future usually take off from generalizations of the past. Of course, Clausewitz's approach may not be relevant to the contemporary theorist. In forming his historical-theoretical point of view, he benefited from a unique congruence of historical, cultural, and intellectual forces that no longer apply today. But even in our age of specialization, which tends to divide knowledge into small parcels, the combination of historical and theoretical interest and purpose is far from rare. Gray, however, emphasizes their mutual exclusiveness: he writes that he is a social scientist, not a historian, that he is "unafraid of big concepts . . . [and] apt to seek and therefore find precedents and parallels across the ages." And he further expands the difference between studying the past and developing theory by firmly declaring, "Historians, cursed as well as blessed by their knowledge, . . . are impaired as a consequence in their ability to empathize with historical figures. . . . Historians are often all but overwhelmed by the rich contextuality of unique events."

These characterizations of what historians do and cannot do are puzzling. They are difficult to square with Gray's admiration of Clausewitz's work, which more than that of any other theorist I can think of, is based on and suffused by the detailed and comparative study of the past. They are also rather one-sided. Gray certainly knows as well as I do that any number of historians have brought together history and theory, the specific with the general, and with this combination exerted a profound impact on Western thought. I need only mention Tocqueville and Burckhardt, both, incidentally, historians whose search for the telling or contradictory detail was linked to deep empathy with (some) individuals they wrote about. But presumably to make a serious point, Gray passed over the many historians who created—and continue to create today—large, even universal patterns out of masses of detail. Some historians *are* blinded by details, just as some theorists are blinded by ignoring them. Those are human weaknesses, however, not weaknesses of the discipline. Still, we are in Gray's debt if his caricature of the historian's shortcomings is meant to alert us to the threat some kinds of specialized thinking pose to broader understanding.

One way to counter this threat may be by bringing disciplines together, and it is my impression that for some time now the interdisciplinary approach has had a strong presence in our thinking about war, past, present, and future, with historians reaching out to other disciplines and social scientists reaching out to history. My personal experience in this field is limited, but in the late 1950s, when I became associated with the Institute for Strategic Study, the various disciplines interacted closely, as a glance at the early issues of its journal *Survival* will show. That was again the case in the internal war project at the Center of International Studies in Princeton, which was headed by Klaus Knorr, originally an economic historian, who during these years wrote two valuable books, *Limited Strategic War* and *Foreign Intelligence and the Social Sciences*. Participants in the internal war project did not always find it easy to make connections across their disciplines, but we learned from each other. The RAND Corporation, when I came to know something about it, had a strong complement of people who thought about war both historically and theoretically: Paul Kecskemeti, for one, and, of course, Bernard Brodie, whom Gray calls "the greatest of modern strategic thinkers." For a time, the head of the social-science division at RAND was the political scientist Alexander George, who with his wife wrote a brilliant historical study on the relationship of President Wilson and Colonel House. When some years later Michael Howard and I invited Brodie to write a commentary for our translation and edition of Clausewitz's *On War*, it quickly became apparent in our conversations and correspondence to what an extent historical events—and, it must be added, historical figures—were among the raw material on which his theoretical ideas and speculations took fire. But though he had a creative, inventive mind, in the breadth of his views he was one among many. Reflecting on the specifics and on the overall character of war, discovering in particular details the indication of general forces that might affect present and future, employing methods from a broad scholarly spectrum—all this was common to many of the historians, social scientists, and theorists in these groups. Far from being alone in his interdisciplinary approach, Gray is in good company, a company extending far back in time, in which large patterns and crucial insights were and continue to be generated, criticized, and tested from different perspectives. Every discipline has within it the potential to set you free.

The Crystal Ball Is Bloody but Still Clear

T. X. Hammes

Colin Gray has nailed it again. His essay "Blood in the Crystal Ball" draws upon history to lay a solid foundation for thinking about the future of war. As a professional defense analyst, he is keenly aware of the incestuous relationships within the defense community among analysts, policy makers, and weapons producers. In particular, he refutes the notion that technology has fundamentally changed warfare.

This may be a bit of a shock to many Americans who have a great faith in technology's transformative effects. For the past fifty-five years, the United States has invested very heavily in maintaining the technological edge in most military fields. This investment has paid off handsomely as some of the Defense Advanced Research Project Agency's wildest dreams have come true. Today, American technology, training, and investment allow U.S. forces to dominate conventional battlefields. Many Iraqi soldiers never even knew they were targeted before they were hit. Based on the "success" there and in Afghanistan, the Pentagon continued to push technology hard, confident that the network-centric future would change the fundamental nature of war. It is only in the last few months that reality has begun to creep into the Quadrennial Defense Review as the Pentagon has acknowledged that enemies may not choose to fight a high-technology war.

Gray scoffs at the idea that a computer will fundamentally change the way war is conducted. He is correct. One of Clausewitz's great insights is "that war is not an exercise of the will directed at an inanimate object, as is the case with the mechanical arts, or at matter which is animate but passive and yielding, as is the case with the human mind and emotions in the fine arts. In war the will is directed at an animate object that reacts."[1] This is a critical point.

From *Historically Speaking* 7 (January/February 2006)

Despite the continuing conflicts in Iraq and Afghanistan, high-technology proponents still assume that the enemy will choose combat against our high-technology forces. They have to do so to justify very expensive network-centric weapons programs such as Future Combat Systems. Yet, because war is an exercise against an animate object that reacts, we know the enemy will seek to avoid our strengths. This is what is happening against the three enemies the United States is fighting today: Iraqi insurgents, Afghan insurgents, and worldwide terrorists. All simply refuse to fight in a way that exposes them to our technology. As thinking enemies, they have moved the contest to terrain that neutralizes our technology. In particular, the Iraqis have used cities to greatly increase the uncertainty and chance of our operations. Thus Gray's firm belief that computers are not fundamentally changing the battlefield is supported not only by history but by current events. Since war is a contest between two opposing wills, we can only measure our combat prowess relative to a specific enemy. Currently we are finding our technology and prowess less than dominating in the types of wars our enemies have chosen to fight.

The purpose of the scenarios proposed in support of the various high-technology weapon systems is not to predict the future as much as to sell a product. Gray makes the very telling point that defense professionals should not be seduced by the promise of a future that plays to U.S. strengths but rather should use both history and current events to understand what the future is likely to bring. There is plenty of evidence that many analysts choose to see the world through the eyes of producers rather than users.

Gray is also correct when he states that we will see major change in the character of some forms of warfare. In fact, we have seen that throughout history. While the fundamental nature of war does not change, the way it is fought evolves along with society as a whole. Changes across the spectrum of political, economic, social, and technical fields bring changes in the way we fight. Obviously the technology of eighteenth-century Europe would not support blitzkrieg, but neither could the economic, social, or political realms. In the same way, many of the combatants in the civil wars raging in Africa have the technology and weapons to fight a war of maneuver but they lack the political and economic organization to do so. As a result, they are reduced to fighting essentially tribal wars.

Gray notes that history is the "only source of evidence on strategic behavior." Success in war requires a strong grasp of history. In addition, because the character of war does change, flexibility is essential. Real flexibility requires both the right organization and the right people. As an American, I find it unfortunate that the Pentagon seems to have this backwards. It is a strongly ahistorical organization that is notoriously inflexible. This may be the single biggest challenge for U.S. strategists: to create flexibility in a huge bureaucracy that has a near monopoly on the U.S. employment of force. Reading Gray's "Blood on the Crystal Ball" is a good place to start.

NOTE

1. Clausewitz, *On War,* ed. and trans. Michael Howard and Peter Paret (Princeton: Princeton University Press, 1984), 149.

Comment on Gray

Victor Davis Hanson

A s a long admirer of Thucydides, I must plead guilty to agreeing with almost all of the sensible points that Colin S. Gray has made. Not long ago in the inaugural issue of the *New Atlantis* (Spring 2003 http://www .thenewatlantis.com/archive/1/hanson.htm), I wrote a brief article entitled "Military Technology and American Culture" that addressed, in the immediate aftermath of the three-week victory over Saddam Hussein, similar misplaced giddiness about the new technology and its role in the perceived "revolution" in war: "The most dangerous tendency of military planners is the arrogant belief that all of war's age-old rules and characteristics are rendered obsolete under the mind-boggling technological advances or social revolutions of the present. Tactics alter, and the respective roles of defense and offense each enter long periods of superiority vis-à-vis each other. The acceptance of casualties is predicated on domestic levels of affluence and leisure. But ultimately the rules of war and culture, like water, stay the same—even as their forms and their pumps change." So I find very little in Gray's essay that I could argue with, inasmuch as he hits on themes of unchanging human nature that sober thinkers such as Angelo Codevilla, Michael Howard, and Donald Kagan have reiterated in warning us about believing that war reinvents itself ex nihilo each generation.

Even the Macedonian sarissas that Gray alludes to in passing are instructive. They did entail a change in tactics (two hands were now required to hold such a long pike, requiring the mostly mercenary phalangites to jettison the old protection of the large hoplite shield held with the left hand) as the phalanx achieved greater killing power (five rows of spear tips, not three, hit the enemy in the initial crash). The sarissa-phalanx's resulting clumsiness necessitated a symphony of forces, as Philip and Alexander protected such

From *Historically Speaking* 7 (January/February 2006)

an unwieldy mass with light and heavy cavalry, the hypaspists, and missile and light-armed troops. Nevertheless, for the men asked to fight, victory was still achieved or lost by the degree of discipline and élan in the ranks, the acumen of their generals who sought out favorable terrain, and the larger political objectives that such forces were used for. In other words, the newfound lethality of the Macedonian phalanx did not change at all the older rules of why men fight, the ingredients for their success or failure, or how such new technology was rightly or wrongly employed in an unchanging strategic landscape.

All of the valuable examples Gray cites from the nineteenth to twentieth century to refute the notion of a radical, technologically based revolution of warfare have earlier antecedents from ancient and medieval times. Catapults were lamented in reactionary literature of the fourth-century b.c. for destroying the old hoplite code predicated on battle courage. But by the century's end, stouter walls, new styles of construction, and counter-artillery mounted on the walls had neutralized even torsion catapults and relegated them to a mere cycle in the age-old tension between the besieger and the besieged.

Fifteenth-century fiery weapons, it is true, soon empowered the offense and eventually made iron, steel, and bronze body plate obsolete. Yet in an age of Kevlar and new ceramics that can stop many bullets, we are relearning not only the age-old science of crafting personal armor but the reasons why such protection is needed when the training and costs of specialist warriors simply make them too expensive to lose. In that sense, Gray is absolutely correct to note: "We do not care about many of the details of warfare's changing character through two and a half millennia. What we care about is the unchanging nature of war."

In this age of materialist thinking, Gray makes an even better point. He quotes Thucydides' famous "fear, honor, and interest" as motivations for war, invoked by the Athenians as the primary reasons that they acquired and kept an empire. The Spartans, Thucydides also says, started the Peloponnesian War out of "fear" (*phobos*) of the growth of Athenian power—since it is hard, despite the many pretexts, to cite any real legitimate grievance against the Athenians who had pretty much kept to the understandings of the existing peace accords. In general, the powder kegs for most wars in the ancient Greek world were ostensibly marginal borderlands, territory of little real economic value but of enormous psychological importance to the perceived collective worth of neighboring agrarian communities.

We constantly need to be reminded of the often-frightening passions of our primordial brains. After September 11 many thought that Osama bin

Laden's earlier fatwas, alleging various grievances—from American troops in Saudi Arabia to the UN oil-for-food embargo of Iraq—were serious writs rather than mere pretexts (Thucydidean *prophases*) for deep-seated anger and humiliation brought on by a globalized and Western culture that really did threaten all the old hierarchies of an increasingly noncompetitive Muslim world. And believing that Osama and his suicide bombers represented some entirely unprecedented existential threat was also as invalid as assuming our cruise missiles or GPS-guided bombs at last offered a lasting antidote to terrorism. In other words, Osama bin Laden probably went to war over a sense of lost honor, in fear of Western globalization, and due to his perceived interest in thinking—given perceptions of relative Western appeasement of radical Islamicist terrorism since 1979—that he could win more than he might lose. And neither his brand of terrorism nor the many antidotes to it were especially novel in the tactical or strategic sense, despite the new technology of miniaturization that allows deadly weapons to be carried on a single person and the computerized-guided weapons that we often use to strike back at terrorist hideouts a half a world away.

My only slight modification of Gray's sensible comments is in regard to his apparent impression that most in the armed forces do not believe as he. Yet I do not think that the defense establishment in toto is quite yet in thrall to the presentism and enslaved by its technological pizzazz. Thucydides and Clausewitz are required reading in many courses at the war colleges and academies, and scores of Defense Department strategic analyses start with the Greeks and Romans. Those with whom I have talked at the Pentagon and in the military are very aware that they are hardly exempt from war's timeless nature simply by reason of their newfangled weaponry but are instead still players in an ancestral deadly game whose age-old truths they must master.

But in general, to believe that Gray is incorrect would be to assume that human nature itself is malleable and that people now act differently than they did in the past—either due to some accelerated evolutionary process that has changed our very brain chemistry since the advent of recorded history or because the use of computers and advanced electronic circuitry alters in some organic fashion the very function of the human brain and its attendant emotions. Thus we would need a new history of a new species to find general truths from the past to guide the future or assume history is bunk because humans alter their genetic makeup and accustomed behavior almost yearly.

In contrast, the extent to which there is real ethical or material progress in human history hinges not merely on technology or new methods of thinking as much as on understanding timeless human nature and the plethora of examples from history that can guide us mutatis mutandis from making the same general mistakes in the present.

My worry, in fact, is not so much with our armed forces and military theorists—who often seem to recognize that the face of war may change but not its essence—as with many of our institutions that ultimately guide and shape civic society.

The general credo, for example, of current peace and conflict-resolution theory programs in American universities is that classical notions of deterrence no longer apply, since either education or evolution can change the nature of man and substitute Enlightenment principles of education and dialogue for the use of credible defenses against primordial enemies. In a recent debate with the peace-studies director at Dartmouth College, I was struck by a comment by Professor Ronald Edsforth, who insisted, "Evolution [of human behavior] is a fact. It didn't stop back in ancient times. . . . We are capable of learning as humans and changing our environment in such a way that that which we abhor is less and less likely."[1]

The problem Gray so ably recognizes may not be that mere defense theorists, generals, and national security advisers are convinced that their new weaponry has invented the world anew. Instead the real worry is that a much larger cast of therapists believes that our dazzling modernity—either by reason of its technology or the evolved humans who created it—is no longer guided by the lessons of the past.

And that is a frightening thought indeed.

NOTE

1. *Dartmouth Review* February 11, 2005. http://dartreview.com/archives/2005/02/11 (accessed September 17, 2007).

History and the Future of War

Antulio J. Echevarria II

M ost historians would probably agree with Colin Gray's contention that future wars will resemble past wars.[1] Many of us have, in fact, been trying for years to get that point across to contemporary defense experts, particularly those possessed by the idea of creating a military revolution based on a few new pieces of technology and several dubious theories. In some cases our points have struck home, but more often they have not. The main reason is not, however, that defense experts or "social-scientist strategists" lack historical perspective, as Gray implies, especially since historians are willing and able to provide them with one. Some of the staunchest advocates of the view that air power is and will continue to be the decisive arm of the future are established historians who certainly do not want for historical perspective. Instead, there are at least two main reasons for our lack of success. First, defense analysts tend to have a vested interest in seeing a theory or concept, usually connected with a particular piece of technology, succeed. Second, the defense business is not about getting ideas right. It's about getting them past the competition and into production. The rewards for success are high. History is, therefore, appealing even to proponents of revolutionary transformation because it can be made to provide the trappings of legitimacy for any number of undeserving concepts, such as network-centric warfare, effects-based operations, and shock-and-awe. Not only do such theories lack an objective basis, such as Clausewitz established for his own theory of war, but their subjective basis—history—is dubious as well. Gray would like to avoid the details that professional historians are wont to embrace, but such a "death by a thousand cuts" is the best, often the only, way to destroy a theory supported by an erroneous historical interpretation. If only it mattered!

From *Historically Speaking* 7 (January/February 2006)

While most historians would agree with the contention that future wars will resemble wars of the past, they would also vigorously disagree with any suggestion that the wars of tomorrow and those of yesterday will not have important differences. For instance, the phenomenon of globalizatio (or the dispersion and democratization of technology, information, and finance) is emerging as a distinguishing feature of the twenty-first century; it is, among other things, increasing the real and virtual mobility of people, things, and ideas, which in turn facilitates the use of terror as a political weapon. Globalization is, of course, hardly the only force shaping the future. A number of important studies identify the growing demand for energy, the proliferation of weapons of mass destruction, and accelerating population growth as among the key trends that are already separating the future from the past.[2] These are the kinds of details historians would find significant, and it is precisely those things strategists need to understand as they apply their skills to future challenges.

If historical experience is the only source of evidence available to us, as Gray believes, then we should certainly approach it soberly. We can approximate the past, as he reminds us. However, we cannot know by any objective measure whether our approximations are 90 percent or 50 percent or 20 percent correct. Ultimately even approximating history comes down to what *feels* right. And that is a function of our training as professional historians and our opportunities to immerse ourselves in the primary sources, whence many of the details come. Leopold von Ranke's famous dictum that the historian's spirit must become one with the spirit that "dwells within the sources" has much to be said for it. The notion of approximating history does not.

My purpose in writing "The Trouble with History," which Gray kindly cites, was twofold: first, to educate students, particularly military students, many of whom approach history with great enthusiasm but little critical thinking, as to what history is and isn't; and, second, to remind my historian colleagues that one of our most important contributions to education is the set of critical thinking skills that history both requires and develops.[3] At the end of the day, we must make our own decisions about what is true regarding the past, just as we must regarding the present. We will rarely have all the facts we require before we making a decision. This is nowhere more true than in the development of strategy.

On one level the article was perhaps too pessimistic, as Gray claims. Yet, on another level it was exactly the opposite, for it reflects my hope that officers and others who might become defense experts would, if armed with a sober appreciation of history and its set of critical-thinking skills, be better equipped to "poach" some of the "sacred beliefs" that pass for theories today. Of course, it is impossible to disabuse genuine zealots of their beliefs. As T. E. Lawrence reportedly said, "An opinion can be argued with; a conviction is best shot." However, as the zealots get their golden parachutes and fade from the defense arena, they just might be replaced by another generation of defense experts more capable of thinking for itself. If Gray can have his illusions about the efficacy of history, I can have mine.

If the future is behind us, the past certainly isn't. Bringing Clausewitz forward, as Gray has done, provides ample evidence of that. I applaud his continued use of the "great Prussian" to help us understand both the nature of war and the essentials of strategy. Of all military works, Clausewitz's *On War* delivers by far the most cogent and considered, if almost too complex, view of the nature of war. Those few defense experts who refer to war's nature tend to do so by drawing from *On War*, though usually only with a quote or two. While Clausewitz's examination of the nature of war teases out those (objective) characteristics common to all wars—such as hostility, chance, and purpose—and those (subjective) qualities that may be unique to each case—such as war's means—his emphasis is on war's variability, not on what is constant. His conclusion is, after all, that the nature of war is both "multifaceted" (*zusammengesetzte*) and "variable" (*veränderliche*).[4] Common elements are not necessarily constant in terms of their values.

Put differently, Clausewitz stressed that war is more than a "simple chameleon" that can alter its external appearance according to its environment; a chameleon can change its color but not its internal composition.[5] War, on the other hand, can vary intrinsically, both in kind as well as by degree. The purposes for which wars are fought, for instance, can range in kind from overthrowing an opponent to arriving at a negotiated settlement. One might begin a war pursuing the former but end it seeking the latter, or vice versa. An intrinsic force, such as, hostility, moreover, could vary in intensity from one war to the next or even multiple times within the same war. Conceivably a change in degree could also be severe enough to make it tantamount to a change in kind. Clausewitz clearly considered the wars of Napoleon—in which hostility reached new levels—substantially different from those of Frederick, where it was not as significant a factor.[6] If the Napoleonic wars represent any kind of revolution in warfare, it was, as he pointed out, due to the changes that occurred in this realm. War thus varies not only in terms of the means used to wage it but also intrinsically with respect to the forces at work within it. This framework and the insights that we might gain in applying it to the present, it seems to me, would ably answer the "quintessential strategist's question, 'So what?'"—that Gray so rightly poses. Hence, any strategist worth his or her salt should care about it.

In short Clausewitz did indeed see all wars as things of the same nature, as Gray points out. However, Clausewitz also saw that nature as variable and its principal elements, even if always present, as continuously in flux. Violence, to offer one example, he described as a "pulsation" (*Pulsieren*), rather than a constant.[7] In any case, if war's common elements were constants, the zealots would be justified in canceling them out of their formulae for success, as indeed they try to do now.

I suspect Gray would agree with this portrayal of the nature of war. My concern, however, is not with his interpretation but how it might be received by those who lack his breadth and depth of knowledge. His argument can be taken as claiming that all one needs to know about the nature of the weather, for instance, is that it consists of a few common and inescapable elements, such as, barometric pressure, heat index, dew point, wind velocity, and so on. This line of reasoning does not allow us to appreciate that there is indeed a qualitative difference between a rain shower and a hurricane—so much so in fact that we might do well to consider them two entirely different types of weather and prepare ourselves accordingly. We ought, therefore, to recognize not only the elements common to all forms of weather but also how those elements relate to each other and how changes in one or more of them will affect how we should prepare ourselves before stepping outdoors.

After all this, I think Gray and I are largely in agreement, except of course on those niggling details.

NOTES

1. The views expressed in this article are the author's own and do not necessarily represent those of the U.S. government.

2. See, for example, the U.S. National Intelligence Council, *Mapping the Global Future* (Washington, D.C.: National Intelligence Council, 2004).

3. Antulio J. Echevarria II, "The Trouble with History in Military Education," *Historically Speaking 7* (September/October 2005): 11–15.

4. Clausewitz, *Vom Kriege* (Bonn: Ferd. Dümmlers Verlag, 1980), book 1, chap. 2, 214.

5. Ibid., book 1, chap. 1, 212–13.

6. Ibid., book 8, chap. 3B, 970–74.

7. Ibid., book 1, chap. 2, 210.

Comment on "Been There! Done That!"

Andrew J. Bacevich

I concur with Colin Gray. Indeed I am almost tempted to say that I agree with every jot and tittle of his essay and to leave it at that. Almost but not quite.

Gray expects others to find his essay "shocking" and "unfashionable" and "controversial." He should prepare to be disappointed. Serious students of war will judge his views to be commonsensical and even conventional. There is not a lot new here. Simplifying only slightly, Gray's argument reduces to a single sentence: "Clausewitz got it about right."

Indeed, he did, especially in fixing the relationship of war to politics. The ugly truth is that as long as politics persists so, too, will large-scale, politically motivated violence. That the innocent, the naïve, and the idealistic will bridle at that prospect is to be expected. As with those who rail against the market or deny the existence of original sin, theirs is an exercise in futility.

To be sure, those opposing all war as a matter of principle serve a useful purpose: they make it harder for ambitious or bloodthirsty politicians to portray the conflict lurking over the horizon as high-minded, moral, and unavoidable. So two cheers for those who protest and demonstrate and proclaim, "Hell no, we won't go." Yet no amount of emoting for peace, however well intentioned, will succeed in making an end to war.

Gray puzzles over the fact that some of those actually in the war business fall prey to their own peculiar version of romanticism. The counterparts to the pacifists denying the utility of war are the visionaries—soldiers as well as strategists—who entertain dreams of perfecting war, liberating it from Clausewitzean risk and uncertainty.

Since the end of the cold war, Americans have shown a particular susceptibility to such fantasies. Theorists have developed any number of PowerPoint

From *Historically Speaking* 7 (January/February 2006)

presentations and published dozens of books and essays teasing out the meaning of the next military "revolution." The Pentagon has published plans that promise to secure for the United States "full spectrum dominance" everywhere and forever. Donald Rumsfeld and his lieutenants prattle on endlessly about the imperatives of "military transformation." In a recent speech, the vice chief of naval operations declared that the defense department's new aim is "overmatch," which he guarantees will enable the United States to "dominate every domain across the phase of war."

At least by the standards of *On War,* little of this qualifies as intellectually serious. To the extent that recent prognostications about war's future are of interest, it derives from what they tell us about the delusions of the age in which we live. In the decades to come, historians will rank the revolution in military affairs right up there with "the end of history," Bill Clinton's "bridge" to the New Millennium, and Thomas Friedman's testimonials on behalf of globalization as symbols of the silliness to which the end of the cold war gave rise.

Politically, the silly season ended on 9/11. Militarily, it ended when the invasion of Iraq produced not a decisive, economical victory but a quagmire that has painfully exposed the limits of American power. Will war's future resemble the past? Yes, that's self-evident. You don't need to rely on Colin Gray for that truth: pick up a newspaper and read the headlines.

Gray may go too far in suggesting that the character of war is "not especially interesting or even important." In a narrow sense, technique matters and can even determine the outcome of a particular conflict. But technique cuts both ways. Innovative methods of combined-arms warfare enabled Germany to defeat Poland and to win the Battle of France—and set Hitler up for the massive miscalculation of Operation Barbarossa. Information technology and precision weapons enabled the Bush administration to handily topple Saddam Hussein—but exaggerated confidence in the efficacy of shock-and-awe set the Americans up for the insurgency that followed.

With Clausewitz to Eternity

Colin S. Gray

This mini-essay is content to consider some points raised by each commentator in turn. More often than not, I find that I wish to endorse and perhaps amplify the points that have been raised.

Several items in Peter Paret's essay require comment. He signals the proclivity of Americans to view their enemies as mirror image of themselves. It is commonplace and not only among Americans to make the convenient assumption that all the world is really one in its strategic thinking. That translates as the comforting belief that all the world shares our ideas and values. This longstanding and pervasive cultural error is now well recognized for the mistake that it is. But recognition of a problem that may be a condition and the consequential correction of perception and subsequent behavior are by no means synonymous. I am much taken with Paret's astute observation that "in war the enemy is often misunderstood and yet may be defeated, and even a malfunctioning political and military leadership may succeed—though presumably success would come at an unnecessarily high cost." Quite so! Fortunately, one does not have to win elegantly or, in the American case, economically. One just has to win. The way that success is secured will have consequences for the postwar political context, so we cannot be indifferent to the skill with which we take down a half-understood enemy. Nonetheless, history tends to be tolerant of the imperfections of those who "win ugly." In practice, all belligerents win or lose more or less ugly.

Paret takes me to task for claiming too deep a division between theorists from the social sciences and historians. He points to the unity of detailed historical research and theory making in Clausewitz's writings. I suspect that the criticism is less well founded than he believes, though I may well have overstated a scholarly divide for the purpose of emphasis. However, I am not inclined to surrender unconditionally and preemptively on this matter. Paret probably underrates the potency and influence of disciplinary bias. It has been my first-hand experience over many years that, unsurprisingly, historians tend to be far better at conducting historical research and interpreting the unique and the particular than they are at relating their findings to some grander narrative. Of course, there are exceptions. There always are. Also, I appreciate that all I am registering here is an impression, albeit one that I have not had cause to alter over a long period. Most scholars attracted to theory will find historical research somewhat confining. The historian's healthy bias toward the unique and the contextual must provide valuable protection against conceptual overreach, windy generalizations, and the like. But the opportunity cost paid in understanding can be heavy.

It is somewhat ironic that Paret picked me up on my claim that Bernard Brodie was "the greatest of modern strategic thinkers." I am not inclined to alter that judgment, but I am pleased to record that the so-called golden age of American strategic thought, from ca. 1954 to ca. 1966, was well populated by some extraordinary talents.[1] By and large, however, those talents were not of the kind celebrated by Paret. If we turn to Brodie's last book, *War and Politics,* we discover an unusually pointed assault upon the suitability of the qualifications of many of his colleagues, especially those at RAND, for the study of strategy. Brodie was highly critical of the prevalence of numerate social scientists among RAND's defense analysts. He was especially unfriendly to the consequences of the skill biases of economists for strategic analysis. Bearing in mind what Paret has to say about the fairly healthy mixture of theory and history among America's strategic theorists, we shall also take note of these words by Brodie: "The usual training in economics has its own characteristic limitations, among which is the tendency to make its possessor insensitive to and often intolerant of political considerations that can get in the way of his theory and calculations. He is normally extremely weak in either diplomatic or military history or even in contemporary politics, and is rarely aware of how important a deficiency this is for strategic insight."

He proceeded to ram home the point by offering the thought that "one is often amazed at how little some of the best-known strategic analysts of our times know about conflicts no more remote in time than World War II, let alone World War I or earlier wars."[2] As if that were not pointed enough, Brodie actually named and shamed some of those he deemed guilty in a footnote that reads as much like a personal, as a professional, comment.[3]

As far as I can tell, from some first-hand knowledge of the principals, RAND in the 1950s and 1960s was a repository of outstanding talents, some scarcely less-outstanding egos, much collaborative scholarship and theorizing, and several culturally distinct tribes of scholars. Brodie complained, I believe with justice, about the narrowness of many of his social-scientific colleagues. There is merit in the old saying, "By their deeds shall ye know them." It was a fact that American "golden age" strategic thinking bore the stamp of economists' rational choices far more prominently than was wise. In each of its three main areas of achievement, deterrence, limited war, and arms control, the new American strategic enlightenment bred what could be called a RAND approach to strategic problems that was as rigorous and as elegant as it was perilously naked of actual historical or cultural context. I will close this brief foray into American strategic thought with a brilliant quotation from Brodie: "Whether with respect to arms control or otherwise, good strategy presumes good anthropology and sociology. Some of the greatest military blunders of all time have resulted from juvenile evaluations in this department."[4] In 2006 the U.S. Armed Forces have finally woken up to the salience of Brodie's advice and warning.[5] There is a problem with context innocent of social-scientific theory and context-dominated historians who are unduly fearful of grand narratives.

I quote Thucydides' peerless trilogy of "fear, honor, and interest" so often in my writings and to students that I fear I am in danger of lessening its authority through the yawn of familiarity induced by undue repetition. We do not know exactly how warfare will be waged in the future or over precisely which issues, but we do know with total confidence that it will be waged for one or more of Thucydides' master motives. Moreover, we can be entirely confident that those motives will be as alive and potent in the twenty-first century as they were in the fifth century B.C. The reason, of course, is traceable with consummate ease to the historical continuity of the human dimension. It would not be quite accurate to claim that the persistence of fear, honor, and interest as galvanizing forces mandate a warlike future. One could argue that those perennial causes of anxiety can and should be met by one or more of the many touted solutions that political and social engineers have invented as substitutes for war. Perhaps we should never say never. War is not a problem to be solved; rather it is a condition to be managed and sometimes an option that needs to be exercised in defense of civilized values.[6]

As must be fully apparent, I find myself in wholehearted agreement with the argument in Victor Hanson's essay. His emphasis on the continuity of the human factor as a—actually *the*—vital spark for and in war, rings especially true.

Colonel Hammes and I are very much of one mind on the strategic utility of technology. All warfare must have a technological dimension. Technology can be essential or useful, or it may be all but irrelevant. It depends on the political, strategic, and military contexts. The issue is not technology per se but rather how it is used. Navies and air forces are utterly dependent on their technology. They ride it into battle. If their machines fail, the warriors fall out of the sky or sink beneath the waves. That granted, it does not follow that the key to decisive victory resides in the toy shops of our high-technology defense industry. Historically speaking, if I dare venture onto alien scholarly turf, there is very little, if any, correlation between a technical edge and victory in war. To push the claim even further, some experts on irregular warfare claim that there is actually an inverse relationship between technological sophistication and success in counterinsurgency.[7] Historically, the simpler the equipment of a counterinsurgency army, the better it has tended to fare in the waging of unconventional struggles.

Recall the maxim that for every solution there is a new problem. Military equipment is procured to fit a rather general notion of the character of future warfare. We do not sustain distinctive armies for different kinds of strategic challenges. The law of the instrument holds that that which is available and with which we feel comfortable will be used. Since, at present at least, the United States does not appear to have a mature and well-understood doctrine for counterinsurgency, it is not exactly well positioned to equip itself most appropriately. The golden rule in counterinsurgency is that the people must be protected as "job one." Chasing bad guys, sweeping aggressively through areas where they are believed to fester, is close to an irrelevance. One does not need the insight of a Clausewitz in order to realize that America's military transformation, focused as it is on incredibly expensive technologies, can hardly fail to encourage faulty doctrine geared to a misunderstanding of the strategic problem.[8]

As Colonel Hammes insists so rightly, America's enemies are obliged to fight smart, because every stupid option would be the path to military and strategic ruin. America's challenge today, as so often in the past, is to settle upon modes of warfare that can deliver not merely military success but rather a favorable strategic and then political decision. In order to do that, one needs first to understand just what one is about and how one's military behavior should translate into the all important currency of strategic effect. An inspired theorist once advised, "The first, the most far-reaching act of judgment that the statesman and commander have to make is to establish by that test [of its political purpose] the kind of war on which they are embarking; neither mistaking it for, nor trying to turn it into, something that is alien to its nature."[9] Our enemies may not succeed in presenting challenges that we cannot meet, but we know that they must and will try to do so. It follows that an effective military establishment for a global superpower must elevate adaptability to pole position as the most essential of its qualities.

I have always maintained that history is cyclical. There is a familiar pattern to my debates with Antulio Echevarria. In its essentials, we tend to open combat from clearly different standpoints, only to discover that our differences are far more apparent than real. I recognize a few familiar themes from our past exchanges in his engaging essay here. Happily, I am pleased to find, as usual, both that I now agree with him, more or less at least, and also that I always did. Nonetheless I am deeply grateful to Echevarria for requiring me to be more careful in my argument than I might have been in the absence of his scholarly overwatch. We social scientists are not always to be trusted on the messy details. There is probably a Chinese proverb that warns that "man with eyes on forest walks into trees." Once we have bought off on an attractive, if flawed, theory we can prove tenacious in its defense. Occasionally, I need to remind myself of Colonel Charles E. Callwell's warning, written a century ago: "Theory cannot be accepted as conclusive when practice points the other way."[10]

Echevarria offers a much-needed reminder to the more scholarly among us that defense issues, including the choice of theory that can add gravitas to doctrine, are rarely, probably never, resolved following a search for some objective truth. As he observes, with some accuracy, "The defense business is not about getting ideas right. It's about getting them past the competition and into production." He should qualify his stricture with the thought that it is often not at all clear just which ideas are "right." To spot and invest reliably in the right ideas requires a measure of foreknowledge that is, alas, not easily obtained. Still, his point is an excellent one. Defense issues are handled in a highly politicized process, which can have immense economic and bureaucratic consequences. There is always a chorus of diverse interests, each tied to a fashionable nostrum or big idea that is held to offer the promise of ever-superior military performance. U.S. defense policy and military strategy are not the result of a process that would pass a fair test of strategic rationality. I must hasten to add that this is a general condition and global phenomenon; it is by no means uniquely American.

Reading Echevarria's essay inclines me to believe that I may well have given an incorrect impression of my respect for historical detail. I suspect that I was so determined to emphasize continuities, especially in the nature of war and strategy, that my somewhat dismissive approach to detail lent itself to misunderstanding. For the record, I am not at all dismissive of tactical detail in any period. But, I do not retreat from my claim, "We [defense professionals] do not care about many of the details of warfare's changing character through two and a half millennia." Why should we? There may be lessons that we should learn from Alexander's battle tactics. In fact I am easily persuaded that that particular combined-arms story is truly instructive.[11] However, I am more interested in Alexander's political and cultural vision, his policy, his grand strategy, and his military strategy. Of course, all of those were enabled only by the prowess of his army at the tactical level. T. E. Lawrence was perceptive, and I believe at least half correct, when he referred to "the whole house of war," wherein strategy and tactics are simply different takes on the same phenomenon.[12] On balance, I regret appearing to be so disdainful of tactical detail.

Echevarria claims, unarguably, I am sure, that "while most historians would agree with the contention that future wars will resemble wars of the past, they would also vigorously disagree with any suggestion that the wars of tomorrow and those of yesterday will not have important differences." I agree completely with him and his fellow historians.

I was amused by Echevarria's useful comments on zealots, and I was pleased to see him deploy one of my favorite quotes from Lawrence. The Lawrentian insight that "an opinion can be argued with . . . [while] a conviction is best shot"[13] is rather close to the mindset and advice currently on offer from the irrepressible Ralph Peters.[14] Echevarria permits himself the hope that today's zealots for false gods of theory "just might be replaced by another generation of defense experts more capable of thinking for itself." Well, I suppose that all things are possible, albeit not equally probable. I should admit that since I have labored for more than thirty years to provide some educational benefit to harassed defense policy makers, I, too, must believe that improvement is possible.

Echevarria insists, fairly persuasively, that Clausewitz emphasizes "war's variability, not . . . what is constant." Echevarria grants that "Clausewitz did indeed see all wars as things of the same nature. . . . However, Clausewitz also saw that nature as variable and its principal elements, even if always present, as continuously in flux." I have no difficulty whatsoever reconciling the Clausewitz who tells us that all wars are "things of the same nature" with the Clausewitz who stresses the high variability of the influence of that nature's essential and unchanging elements.[15] So, what is in dispute here, if anything? I think that Echevarria errs in taking a sound idea too far. If I dare venture the heretical thought, it is entirely possible that both Echevarria and Clausewitz overstate an excellent argument. Echevarria claims, perhaps accurately, "Clausewitz also saw that nature [of war] as variable." On reflection, I believe that Clausewitz inadvertently gave the false impression that the variability of war's eternal components meant that war had a variable nature. I do not believe that the great man endorsed such a strange notion. In my view, all that Clausewitz claimed was that the elements always present in war, most especially his trinity of passion, chance, and reason, will vary immensely from war to war, even from occasion to occasion, in their relative influence on events. To my mind, at least, assuming that I am not doing undue violence to the theory, what Clausewitz describes does not amount to a claim that war has a variable nature.

Echevarria's analogy between my view of the nature of war and a hypothetical, essentialist, simpleminded approach to understanding global weather is, of course, more than a little unfair as well as being inaccurate. However, the analogy does incline me to reconsider my position. It may just be that I have been overly rigid in my understanding of war's permanent nature. Certainly, I agree with him in the need to recognize radical differences among conflicts. Can it be that the high variability of the salience of war's enduring features is more significant than is its eternal nature per se? Having just written those words, which could challenge what I have long believed, I must confess that despite some honest endeavor here, I remain unconvinced that I was wrong.

After braving the shot and shell from Echevarria and emerging, I believe intact, but admittedly a little shaken, it remains only for me to record my general agreement with the characteristically robust commentary by Andrew Bacevich. Alas, he is all too correct when he states, dismissively, "To the extent that recent prognostications about war's future are of interest, it derives from what they tell us about the delusions of the age in which we live." Harsh, but generally perceptive and plausible. With justice, he picks me up on my unduly casual suggestion that the character of war is "not especially interesting or even important." I should not have said that. The character of war does matter, and it always will. The character of war will shape, even determine, the character of the peace that follows. Since war is only about that peace, the way the war is fought, indeed the myriad details of a conflict, cannot fail to be of the greatest importance.

NOTES

1. To the best of my knowledge, I was the originator of the thesis that there was a golden age of American strategic thought from ca. 1954 to ca. 1966. See Colin S. Gray, *Strategic Studies and Public Policy: The American Experience* (Lexington: University Press of Kentucky, 1982), chap.4. The thesis has yet to be challenged.

2. Bernard Brodie, *War and Politics* (New York: Macmillan, 1973), 474–75.

3. Ibid.

4. Ibid., 332.

5. See Robert H. Scales Jr., "Culture-Centric Warfare," *Naval Institute Proceedings* 130 (September 2004): 32–36.

6. For my most recent scholarly joust with a very big idea that has been designed ultimately to retire war from the human experience, see Colin S. Gray, "Sandcastle of Theory: A Critique of Amitai Etzioni's Communitarianism," *American Behavioral Scientist* 48 (2005): 1607–25.

7. Ian F. W. Beckett and John Pimlott, eds., *Armed Forces and Modern Counter-Insurgency* (New York: St. Martin's, 1985), 10.

8. I develop these somber thoughts at some length in *Irregular Enemies and the Essence of Strategy: Can the American Way of War Adapt?* (Carlisle, Pa.: U.S. Army War College, 2006).

9. Carl von Clausewitz, *On War,* ed. and trans. Michael Howard and Peter Paret (Princeton: Princeton University Press, 1976), 88.

10. Charles E. Callwell, *Small Wars: A Tactical Textbook for Imperial Soldiers* (1906; London: Greenhill, 1990), 270.

11. See David J. Lonsdale, *Alexander, Killer of Men: Alexander the Great and the Macedonian Art of War* (London: Constable, 2004).

12. T. E. Lawrence, *Seven Pillars of Wisdom: A Triumph* (New York: Doubleday, 1991), 191–92.

13. Ibid., 190.

14. Ralph Peters, "In Praise of Attrition," *Parameters* 34 (Summer 2004): 24–32.

15. Clausewitz, *On War,* 606.

PART 3

Soldiering and the Experience of War

The British Soldier Then and Now

An Interview with Richard Holmes

Richard Holmes is one of Britain's leading military historians. He was a member of the Department of War Studies at the Royal Military Academy Sandhurst between 1969 and 1985, when he left to command Second Battalion, the Wessex Regiment. In 1995 he became professor of military and security studies at Cranfield University. In 1999 he became colonel of the Princess of Wales's Royal Regiment. He is perhaps best known for *Acts of War: The Behavior of Men in Battle* (1986) and *Soldiers: A History of Men in Battle* (1986), a companion book to the prizewinning BBC TV series, with John Keegan. Holmes has completed a trilogy on the history of the British soldier: *Redcoat: The British Soldier in the Age of Horse and Musket* (2002), *Tommy: The British Soldier on the Western Front, 1914–1918* (2004), and *Sahib: The British Soldier in India, 1750–1914* (2006). In addition he has just published a book on Iraq, *Dusty Warriors: Modern Soldiers at War* (2007). *Historically Speaking* editor Donald A. Yerxa interviewed him on August 5, 2005.

DONALD A. YERXA: You wrote *Tommy* at least in part because you were dissatisfied with the way the First World War on the Western Front has been remembered and narrated. What is the nature of your dissatisfaction, and how does *Tommy* address this?

RICHARD HOLMES: My first problem is that most of us here in the United Kingdom come to the war as literature before we come to it as history. And if I am talking to a school audience, I can be sure they have read Wilfred Owen's poems in Eng Lit before they've read any history on the war. The war has become a literary event more than a historical event, and that worries me.

From *Historically Speaking* 7 (November/December 2005).

I happen to be a fan of the Siegfried Sassoon trilogy, but it postdates the war by quite a long time. The second problem is that we've tended increasingly to want a reason for the war and the loss of life. The war cost Britain and its empire one million dead. It's the first really big, costly war that we Brits fought—more costly even than the Second World War. We look at it like an iron gate that separates the past from the present. And we want a reason for how this happened and why our politicians and commanders let us in for it. So there has been a great tendency to see the war in terms of what I call the "donkeys school" of historiography [from the cliché that the British army consisted of lions led by donkeys]—that is to say generalship, for and against. There are writers who write perfectly respectable books about generals and never address private soldiers.

The final issue has to do with the fact that this was a very literate army. Soldiers wrote letters; they kept diaries. These were often middle-class men who wrote about what they thought. It seems that if we want to understand the war, we ought to go back to what the soldiers told us about it. And in Britain there is no excuse for not doing that. There are two great burgeoning archives—one in the Imperial War Museum in London and another in the Liddle Collection at the University of Leeds—full of material and expanding so quickly that a working historian can barely keep track of it. And I wanted to go back to what they told us about what they were doing. There are dangers in this because no doubt people are not going to tell their mothers everything about how things were. But despite this danger, there is immediacy and poignancy to a diary entry written by someone who doesn't know whether he's going to be alive at tea time.

YERXA: You note that "writers often paint a picture that the men of 1914–18 would look at with disbelief." How should we remember the Tommies of the Western Front?

HOLMES: We should remember them the way that they saw themselves. I sometimes grow impatient with historians who see these soldiers as victims, helpless figures sent off to their destruction. That's not the way that a lot of them thought of themselves. We ought to remember them as part of the biggest collective endeavor in British history. This was the largest army we have ever put into the field, the largest single thing we have ever done. Right or wrong—I'm not trying to defend or attack the war—they were people who by and large were prepared to do what a later generation might call their patriotic chore and often did it to the best of their ability. What we miss in so many accounts were the essentials of this generation, their rough humor, their enormous sense of endurance, their almost apolitical confidence in their nation (this wasn't a flag-waving patriotic generation but a generation that had a profound subpolitical belief that somehow Britain was right and others wrong). It's the sense of humor, toughness, and confidence that we often don't see in accounts written about the war. And that is something I think they would resent. They would resent us not remembering that they liked to sing songs and go to the music hall with its comic and slightly near-the-knuckle [risque] songs. They loved football. Theirs was a football-playing army. If you stopped for a minute, someone would get a ball, and there would be a kickabout. The soldiers were deferential but with an edge. And this rich mixture of sentiments and habits often doesn't come out in our histories of the war.

YERXA: Max Hastings argued in *Overlord* that man for man, the German army was the best in the Second World War and in *Armageddon* that the Germans and Russians in that conflict were better warriors but worse human beings than British and American soldiers. How would you characterize the British Tommy in WWI compared to his French, German, and American counterparts?

HOLMES: The big difference is with the French and the Germans. We must remember that at the outset this was not a conscript army. It is a key ingredient of British history that we have always tended—as indeed has the United States—to have armies that are volunteer not conscripted. That colors a lot. In the French and German armies you had conscription and obligatory military service before the war, and as a consequence, the idea of military service as a civic obligation was deeply entrenched. The French and German armies were a pretty reasonable social cross-section even when the war started. You can reconstruct this in a variety of ways. In both these armies, noblemen served as private soldiers, but in the British army, that would be regarded as impossible, though I can provide one example toward the end of the war. Until very late in the war, the British army was not a microcosm of British society. Both the French and the German armies were large at the beginning of the war and trained on the basis of being big armies, whereas the British army had always engaged in what we might call "the small change of war." One of the reasons why the British army had problems in big battles like the Somme and Passchendaele is that it got big at exactly the same time as it learned its craft. If you had gone to a British platoon at the end of the war and asked if anyone was there in 1914, it would be very surprising if anyone put their hand up. If you went to a French or German platoon and asked the same question, you would inevitably find some people who were there in 1914. The British army in the war was a balloon inflated by volunteers and wartime conscripts with a very thin outer skin composed of people with prewar military experience. The American army was more similar to the British army than either the French or German armies. The American army was expanding very quickly, and the war ended before it could reach its maximum efficiency. The U.S. Army in its brief time of the Western Front was confronting precisely the problems the British had encountered and, with much pain and many casualties, largely overcome. Both were small armies that got too big too quickly.

YERXA: There are some military historians who emphasize the contributions of citizen soldiers as a component to a distinctively "Western way of war." Does your work with British soldiers confirm this?

HOLMES: Interestingly, the British have never felt comfortable with the notion of a citizen soldier. In France, the idea of military service was a two-way street. It was something that not only produced trained soldiers but also respectable citizens. I don't think Britain bought into that before the war. We were always slightly suspicious of soldiers, who by definition were almost always regulars and, to generalize, people who joined the army because there was nothing else to do. We didn't look at soldiers and say, "Here is a member of society we can make more useful by carrying out this civic duty." More likely we'd say, "Now we've got somebody who if given the chance might molest our daughters and take our sons drinking." The American military experience was different yet again because of the relatively recent legacy of the American Civil War. So I am cautious in the British context of seeing a link between military service and civic duty. I started my career as a French-military historian, and I can remember cutting my teeth on documents that enthusiastically made this link. And this was not the sort of thing that you would find the British talking about before the First World War.

YERXA: How well did the British Army handle the complicated task of transforming a small peacetime force into the large army of 1917–1918?

HOLMES: Eventually it did it well enough, but to understand the history of the British army in the war, you have to put this at the very front of your thought process. This is an army that went from having a quarter-million regulars and another quarter-million territorials in 1914 [the Territorial Force replaced the old militia in 1908] to putting over five million men through the army. Inevitably this created difficulties, all the more so because it wasn't planned. Had it been planned I dare say the British army might have made better use of its regulars in 1914. Thousands of men were killed or wounded who would have provided the skeleton and central nervous system for the new army. The British army lost more than half of its staff-trained officers in the first year of the war. When they started raising the new army, they got extraordinary numbers of men to join. For example on September 3, 1914, alone, thirty-three thousand men joined the army. That's incredible. But these men had got no uniforms, no rifles, no ammunition for the rifles they hadn't got. They had got no rifle ranges on which to fire the ammunition they hadn't got for the rifles they didn't possess. The same is true for their newly raised gunners [artillery]: there were no field guns, no heavy guns, no medium guns, no horses to pull the guns, no ammunition, and no ranges— no ability to train gun crews or artillery observers. This would have been an extraordinary task had there been no war going on, but they had to do all this at the same time they had to identify and react to what was happening on the Western Front. For the British and Americans, it was a two-fold task: the radical and unplanned increase of an army to fight in a war that in itself was producing radical change. I don't think we did it perfectly, but we didn't do it as badly as we might have done.

YERXA: How do you assess the leadership of the British Army on the Western Front?

HOLMES: First World War British generals are hard to like. Consider the way that Gary Sheffield and John Bourne's excellent recent edition of Field Marshal Haig's diaries have been reviewed.[1] Most reviewers tend to say, "Great book, awful subject." No matter how hard you try, it is difficult to make people like First World War generals. We are in so many ways prejudiced against them. But, in fact, they were not much worse and probably not much better than most of their allies and opponents. Haig was right to recognize that the Western Front was where the war would be decided. I can see no alternative to the Western Front, and I think he was right to concentrate on that. By the end of the war, Britain produced some very competent divisional commanders and a few competent corps commanders. But we must always remember they were producing them from a very small core. In the British army we did not produce a single reservist—or amateur, if you like, someone commissioned during the war—to command a division on a permanent basis. And certainly no corps commanders other than from the regular army. It is interesting that both the Australian Corps commander, Sir John Monash, and the Canadian Corps commander, Sir Arthur Currie, were territorials (citizen soldiers or militiamen). These corps were among the best on the British side. And it seems to me—without looking for conspiracies— that the regular army did keep the golden gift of high command in its own hands. Maybe we could have done better if we had looked more widely. The British were selecting their high commanders from a tiny pool. And if you took any profession—literary editors, writers, postmen, school teachers—and wanted to increase the size of the leadership out of the existing recruited pool, you would inevitably find some good, some bad, and some indifferent. That's what we find with British generalship in the First World War.

YERXA: *Tommy* is filled with moving accounts of courage and endurance. Is there one example that you encountered in your research that stands out?

HOLMES: There is one example of bravery that I always come back to. There were two members of a battery of field artillery (134th Battery RFA) at the third battle of Ypres in the summer of 1917. One was a junior non-commissioned officer, Acting Lance Bombardier Fisher; the other Gunner Monchie. These two were the only people on the gun line of their battery who survived an attack by gas and shell. Everyone about them was dead or wounded. Fisher and Monchie brought their gun into action to support the infantry, and the two of them sustained a creeping artillery barrage until help came, and Fisher, who was badly gassed, was carried away. That episode has always struck me. These guys never received Victoria Crosses, they were not in the public gaze, and they don't appear in many books. Two young men fighting in the mud with their gas masks on, not held to their task by any external discipline. Who would have noticed had they abandoned their gun? This is the coolest kind of courage: sticking about your job when all about you are the dead and wounded, because the infantry expect it of you. That's the way I'd like to remember British soldiers of the First World War—not being the first man over the top of the trench but sticking to it, doing the business because you were held together by bonds of mateship and because you are the public face of your unit. And you would die rather than let it be shamed.

YERXA: *Tommy* is a sequel to *Redcoat: The British Soldier in the Age of Horse and Musket* (2002). How far off the mark have screen depictions of the redcoat been in movies like *Rob Roy, Last of the Mohicans,* and *The Patriot?*

HOLMES: You have struck a raw nerve. They are far off the mark. I am profoundly concerned by the way Hollywood depicts history. Across the board what it is after is a story. The most extreme example regarding this is the massacre in the church in *The Patriot*. Well, it didn't happen. You cannot say that it was exaggerated. *It did not happen!* King George's soldiers in North America did some bad things, but they didn't crowd people into a church and set fire to it. The view that this is some metaphor for war's frightfulness isn't good enough. Hollywood goes for the easy hit, the easy characterization of Cornwallis, with the two dogs. He wasn't like that at all. By the end of the War for American Independence, the two armies looked very similar, and they had a nucleus of regular soldiers—our redcoats and your continental line. The continental line was as important, if not more, an instrument of patriot victory than the minutemen ever were. But we drearily go back to the assumption that all Brits wore red coats and fought in lines, and all Americans were jolly patriots who skirmished about with rifles. So the redcoat has been a particularly easy target. And I would say that, wouldn't I? The purpose of hauling him halfway across the world is usually to get him to attack an enemy position shoulder to shoulder and to do it methodically. But there was certainly more texture to the guy than we often see. The minute that Hollywood puts its finger on anything, texture goes, and the obvious comes in.

YERXA: From an American perspective, it would seem that one of the greatest challenges in writing about British soldiers' lives is the decentralized structure of the British army. With so many regiments having distinctive traditions and practices, is it difficult to make generalizations?

HOLMES: The British army is indeed distinctively heterogeneous. It still isn't a unified army in what you would regard as an obvious sense. We are in the middle of a great row about restructuring our regiments even as we speak. I'm sure it is not an issue that would cause much comment anywhere else in the world. To understand the British army, you need to understand that the soldier lives on a complicated little street. And on the street all the houses (regiments) look different. It's awfully easy to give him the same street address but forget that each house is very different: it has its own approach, its own clientele, it does things in its own way. So I suppose one problem is coping with this. But if you are coming to it from a Brit military background, as I do, then you understand the diversity, and it's no problem for you.

I suppose a bigger problem over here is writing for a readership that is more demilitarized than it has ever been. The interested general reader may not know the difference between a brigadier and a bombardier, a battalion and a brigade. The familiarity with the way an army does business that would have existed twenty-five years ago now simply doesn't exist. My readers often perceive the people I am writing about as figures in an alien landscape. Now—and this is a very British thing—I am colonel of the Princess of Wales's Royal Regiment, which means that I am, if you like, the nonexecutive chairman of a regiment of infantry (two regular battalions and a reserve battalion). And I had the pleasure of spending some of last summer with my first battalion in a place called al-Amarah, between Basra and Baghdad. One of our soldiers, Private Johnson Beharry, won the Victoria Cross, the highest award in the British military and our equivalent to your Congressional Medal of Honor. He is the first living recipient of the VC since 1969. Wearing my two hats, of military officer and military historian, it struck me how very much the people I visited in Iraq resembled the people I was writing about, how comparatively little the nature of the British soldier has changed. Of course, they look different because we are a far more multiracial society than we once were, but they are kept together by the same qualities. Their rough humor, for example, is much the same. And I had a remarkable sense of déjà vu. History has not stopped. Here are people made brave by the same things, worried about the same things; these are soldiers just like the ones I've spent the last part of my academic career writing about.

In fact I am writing a book about just this. I was struck by how very much they deserved to be explained to the population that has produced them. I'm not sure whether there is this problem in America, but over here we have a small professional army that is seen almost like a bunch of itinerant plumbers. They are sent off to some distant part of the world to do a difficult and potentially smelly job. We like to keep the bathroom door shut because we don't really want to know what's going on inside, and we want them to emerge later with the washers fixed and not too many knuckles skinned and no unpleasant smells. We aren't terribly good at really wanting to know what it is like for them and what they have to do on our behalf. As a historian, I hope I have been reasonably successful explaining that. And I now find myself doing it for those people fighting in Iraq last summer.

YERXA: In the mid-1980s you wrote about the behavior of soldiers in battle: *Acts of War* and, with John Keegan, *Soldiers*. More recently in *Tommy* and *Redcoat*, you have focused specifically on the British army and have seemingly shifted emphasis a bit from the experience of combat to ordinary soldiers' lives. Was such a shift intentional? And, if so, does it relate to broader trends in the field of military history?

HOLMES: I have to say that before your question I didn't know that I made such a shift. But perhaps I have. If so, it wasn't a conscious desire on my part to give up writing operational military history. I did not come to the conclusion that I will write no more books on battles. Nor do I think that there is a particular trend of which this is a part. Max Hastings's *Armageddon: The Battle for Germany, 1944–1945* and Anthony Beevor's *Stalingrad* and *Berlin: The Downfall, 1945* have all sold well over here. For reasons that I cannot identify, I became more interested in the social side of military history. But that happened without a Damascus Road conversion. Before I started *Redcoat*, I decided that I wanted to write three books telling the story of the British soldier across different portions of history and that they should be thematic not chronological. The first two, *Redcoat* and *Tommy*, have done rather well. And I'm really sanguine about the next one, *Sahib: The British Soldier in India, 1750–1914,*[2] which will come out very soon. So I cannot claim that I was following some grand historiographical scheme. I am a historian who is in this as much for his heart as his head. My heart pushes me in a certain direction, and my brain follows.

YERXA: How do you assess the present state of the field of military history?

HOLMES: When I started teaching military history, I was part of a small and endangered species. The minute I stuck my head out of my burrow, a high-velocity round cracked past it. The assumption was that military history was not a valid subject and that people who studied it subscribed to Prussian values. The way that it was all headed was toward war studies, international relations, and even peace studies. In the 1960s military history looked to be endangered. Over the years, the situation has improved. Military history, at least in the UK, has become wholly respectable. You can do some first degrees in it over here, though there is a debate as to whether it is a proper subject for a first degree. And I think we have established the fact that military history needn't be part of a broader thing called war studies. It is a perfectly proper part of history. Certainly military history ought to be a broad church. I commend people who write operational military history as much as I commend people who work in social military history. The subject of my work has been one of mankind's most passionate dramas. Whether it is a drama that we should witness as often as we do is another issue. But it is something we need to know more about. And we owe it to the actors in these dramas to understand war better. If we look at the practice of military history as it has evolved in our lifetime, I think we understand wars and warriors better than we did twenty-five years ago. But that understanding is more narrowly focused among those who are more interested in it rather than across the entire population. And I regret that.

YERXA: Who has influenced your work the most?

HOLMES: Like most British military historians of my generation, I was extraordinarily influenced by Sir Michael Howard. In the 1960s when I was doing my first degree at Cambridge, he was the doyen of military history in this country. He was the person to whom one looked to as a guide in so many ways. He had just published his wonderful book on the Franco-Prussian War. I try to visit the battlefields of that war once every year, and I take Howard's book with me. That book, written in the mid-1960s, has aged so very well. It still delights me as much now as when I first read it. So I was enormously influenced by him, and I was lucky enough to have him as an external examiner when I did my doctorate. The second person who has influenced me is someone who is far less well known, though he ought to be equally well regarded. His name is Christopher Duffy, and he taught military history at the Royal Military Academy Sandhurst when I was there. He earned a doctorate from Oxford, and he is an old-fashioned scholar with an extraordinary ability to read almost all European languages. He has produced a stunning series of books, concentrating mainly on fortification and the armies of the eighteenth century. One of the delights of working at Sandhurst—it had numerous "undelights" as well—was being able to chat with Christopher over coffee each morning and to pick that massive brain of his. I am never ashamed to admit that throughout my career I have depended hugely on the wisdom of my elders and betters. Nowadays it's my own graduate students who stimulate me with great ideas. People ask why I don't make my living entirely by my pen, and I respond that I teach because I love it and because it brings me into contact with distinguished colleagues and bright students.

YERXA: What are you working on now?

HOLMES: *Sahib* is finished, and by the time this interview appears, it will be in print. And it will look very much like *Redcoat* and *Tommy:* a thematic treatment of the British soldier, this time in India, 1750–1914. By the British soldier, I mean British mercenaries working for Indian princes, the British East India Company's officers and men, and regular-army regiments serving in India. I hope to finish very soon a book about Iraq.[3] This is not a history of the Iraq war or Richard Holmes's views on the war. This is a book about 650 men in a battalion of the Princess of Wales's Royal Regiment in a hot and steaming Iraqi town for six months doing a particular job. It is based partly on my own observation. But since I was only there for a short time, it is based far, far more on what these soldiers have written. I have private accounts from the battalion commander down to private soldiers, who would not ordinarily see themselves as literary types, talking about this strange sort of war where you are delivering humanitarian supplies on one block, enforcing the peace on another block, and fighting high-intensity war on a third block. The book is an anatomy of a single battalion in a single bit of Iraq at a particular point in our history. And I'm writing it because I think they deserve to be written about. The surprise for me and some of the elder members of the battalion—people like the company sergeant majors and company commanders—was how good the PlayStation generation is. These are the guys that before they were in the army used to cause trouble on the street corners, wear hooded jackets, etc. But when you see them in Iraq, they are magic. And the older soldiers wanted me to relay how good, how comradely, how brave, how restrained these young soldiers are, and how much their story deserves to be told—which is why I am writing the book.

NOTES

1. Gary Sheffield and John Bourne, eds., *Douglas Haig: War Diaries and Letters, 1914–1918* (London: Weidenfeld and Nicholson, 2005).

2. *Sahib: The British Soldier in India, 1750–1914* (New York: HarperCollins, 2006).

3. *Dusty Warriors: Modern Soldiers at War* (New York: HarperPerennial, 2007).

No Quarter

The Pacific Battlefield

Eric Bergerud

World War II was, by a great margin, the most violent conflict in modern times. Yet Japanese and American soldiers fought the land war in the Pacific with a savage and relentless intensity that was rarely equaled and never surpassed in World War II. Although it is possible to identify incidents of restraint and humanity coming from both sides, the essence of the conflict was something very close to a war of annihilation.

The grim nature of the Pacific War is best illustrated by the extremely low number of prisoners taken. The numbers tell a dismal tale. Approximately thirty-seven thousand Japanese servicemen surrendered during land operations in the Pacific War. This was opposed to a total of killed in action that surpassed one million. In other words, for every Japanese soldier or sailor fighting on land (Japan had no marine corps and the naval personnel were involved in all major ground campaigns) that surrendered, there were twenty-five killed. In comparison, in northwest Europe both Britain and U.S. ground forces lost one prisoner for every two men killed. But the numbers are even worse than they seem. A very high percentage of Japanese POWs surrendered in the waning months of the Pacific War in areas such as the South Pacific or the Philippines where imperial garrisons had long been isolated. Men were starving, in despair, and military discipline gone. What was absent, however, was an organized surrender of a large number of prisoners during or at the end of any of the major land campaigns, the kind of occurrence that was typical in every other theater of war. After the surrenders of several garrisons early in 1942, almost no American soldiers or marines

From *Historically Speaking* 3 (June 2002)

became prisoners and lived to tell the tale. In short, when the Japanese and Americans squared off in battle, there was no quarter asked or given.

The most common explanation for what John Dower called "War without Mercy" is racial hatred between the Japanese and Americans. Although Japan receives a share of the blame, deeply ingrained Western racism, as manifested in the United States, is found to be the prime culprit. Scholars attempt to prove their point with a cavalcade of propaganda posters, films, cartoons, and articles in the press. The Japanese were systematically portrayed as animals; consequently, so goes the argument, extermination was a natural response to Japan's attack. Many now argue that wartime propaganda campaigns in the West were only one manifestation among many of an old pattern of racist behavior that created the slave trade, underlay colonial empires, and led to the incarceration of thousands of Japanese citizens in the United States in 1942. I don't doubt that ethnic loathing was part of the equation. However, for a number of reasons, I find this argument incomplete.

One problem is obvious. If the murderous nature of combat in the Pacific was generated by American or Western racial attitudes toward Asians, it is very difficult to explain why U.S. forces took huge numbers of POWs in the Korean War. If racial enlightenment had taken place, or the rules of engagement within the U.S. military had changed between 1945 and 1950, I find it difficult to detect. Likewise, in Vietnam, Americans captured enemy soldiers in numbers that dwarfed those of the Pacific War.

We should also remember that there was no history of conflict between Japan and the United States. Nor were American soldiers fighting for the physical survival of the United States. Many in America's intellectual class had long found much to admire in Japan, although Japanese aggression against China did much to tarnish Tokyo's image. More important, the segment in the American political arena that wished either to enter World War II or become more actively involved had its eyes on the struggle against Hitler. Although conspiracy theorists continue to try to prove otherwise, I am convinced that Washington very much wanted peace in Asia as long as Japan did not threaten Western interests in Southeast Asia.

I doubt such calculations had much impact on the young men swept up into war. Eighteen- or twenty-year-olds of 1941 were no less apolitical or self-possessed than their contemporaries of today. I have spent the last seven years researching the Pacific War and have interviewed about two hundred veterans of all services, mostly American. I asked each about their attitudes toward the Japanese. When describing their wartime service, almost all expressed retrospective hatred: many admitted that the hatred had not totally cooled over a half century. Interestingly, however, many GIs pointed out that prior to service in the Pacific, they had never met a Japanese person or an American citizen of Japanese descent. These same men admitted that they knew almost nothing about Japan. Obviously, Pearl Harbor changed this situation overnight. It is also clear, in my view, that these men learned their hatred not at home but on the battlefield.

It is important to realize that American servicemen heading to war in 1942 lacked any systematic political indoctrination. Whatever racial attitudes existed in society, there was no "hate Japan" curriculum in the public schools. Prior to Pearl Harbor, political indoctrination within the armed services was forbidden because it would arouse the ire of isolationists. The young men who swamped recruiters after December 7 received the most cursory of training before being shipped out to destinations like Guadalcanal. (Some Marines I interviewed recall receiving weapons training onboard troop transports en route to the South Pacific.) In such conditions there was no time for indoctrination or systematic propaganda. By the time the U.S. government, aided by Hollywood, did create a formidable propaganda machine, the Pacific battlefield had already been poisoned by bitter experience, not political manipulation.

The war of annihilation that marked the Pacific War resulted from unique battlefield dynamics. In other words, the slaughter was homegrown in the Pacific jungles rather than a reflection of outside social influences. To understand this violent dynamic, it is important to understand how surrender is handled on the battlefield. At that time, the concept of surrender was accepted by every army in the world. Even Imperial Japanese forces took prisoners. This reflected tacit recognition that when violence was separated from military purpose, it became either murder or suicide. It also stemmed from powerful self-interest. If a soldier knows the enemy will take prisoners, he is far more likely to give up. If he believes he will die regardless, he fights on. Most armies wish to end battles as quickly as possible with minimal losses and welcome surrender. They realize, however, that this is a reciprocal relationship. If one side takes prisoners, so must the other.

In practice, surrender entails great danger on the battlefield. Surrender is much safer if it is done by several people at once and with some type of prearrangement. Once fighting starts, the situation changes drastically. If machine gunners start a fight, inflict casualties on the other side, and then decide they wish to surrender, they are facing likely death. If they are powerful enough, the enemy might accept surrender out of simple self-preservation. If not, the code of battle allows men to take retribution. If one side has committed an atrocity, the chances for safe surrender by its soldiers also declines greatly. Consequently, surrender should be viewed as a tacit pact. It is done to avoid mutual violence and breaks down in the midst of bloodshed. This is true in all wars. Killing the helpless was not unique to the Pacific.

The most remarkable behaviors shown by Japanese soldiers were their willingness to accept orders that meant certain death and their refusal to surrender. To what extent the Japanese soldier's willingness to recklessly embrace death reflected something deep in Japanese culture I will let others judge. However, it is undeniable that a Japanese youth in 1941, very much unlike his American counterpart, had been subject to intense military indoctrination in and out of the education system. Present in some form from the start of the Meiji era, the propaganda barrage reached a fever pitch in the late 1930s. In short every Japanese soldier was imbued with a kind of ersatz *bushido* that bound the individual to the state and glorified death in battle as the supreme act of sacrifice and spiritual purification.

Every Japanese serviceman possessed a copy of the Emperor Meiji's famous Imperial Edict of 1882. It contains a striking image. The cherry blossom, beloved of the Japanese, falls to earth in perfect form. The edict counsels, "If someone should enquire of you concerning the spirit of the Japanese, point to the wild cherry blossom shining in the sun." Thus, the Japanese honored the sanctity of the death of the young in battle. The death of the young is one face of war. Unfortunately for all concerned, the Japanese veneration of death was unique and came dangerously close to becoming a cult of oblivion. It struck at the very nature of the warrior code as understood in the West. The Japanese viewed the idea of surrender, accepted widely in the West, as a sign of weakness. Unfortunately, if Japanese officers did not hallow the lives of their own soldiers, they likewise showed a contempt for the lives of the foe. It was this terrible chemistry that made Pacific battlefields killing grounds of unusual ferocity.

American soldiers learned very quickly that combat in the Pacific would be unlike that engaged in during any previous war. Pearl Harbor itself had enraged the nation and was living proof that the Japanese could not be trusted. As the first American expeditionary force of the Pacific War headed to Guadalcanal, rumors were already circulating of Japanese cruelty in the Philippines and on Wake Island. Officers were also telling their young soldiers that the Japanese did not surrender. Japanese victories had also given American soldiers a healthy respect for their enemy's fighting skills. Thus fear also was added to the brew.

Dire predictions of a brutal war proved true in America's first two Pacific campaigns—Guadalcanal and Buna. In both of these campaigns—fought nearly simultaneously during the fall of 1942 through the early winter of

1943—an alarming pattern developed. Japanese forces showed astounding courage during both attack and defense. However, Japanese tactical doctrine, which relied so heavily on the fanatical spirit of the individual infantryman, ultimately proved wanting in face of Allied fighting skill and superior firepower.

Now it is safe to say that any general wants his army to fight with courage in the face of bad odds. The Japanese soldier fulfilled this duty to the fullest in the Solomons and in New Guinea. In both battles Imperial forces inflicted serious losses and cost the Allies valuable time. Unfortunately, during the concluding stage of both battles, the Japanese battle ethos degenerated into a completely pointless waste of life, most of it Japanese. By January 1943, the Japanese were facing a hopeless position at both Guadalcanal and Buna. Recognizing this, the Japanese high command evacuated some twelve thousand men from Guadalcanal. However, this still left several hundred Japanese infantry manning positions in a ridgeline south of Henderson Field that the Americans called Mount Austen. These soldiers were isolated, starving, and in miserable physical condition. They had done their duty and should have surrendered. Instead, in every case, these garrisons fought to the last man, often ending resistance in a pointless but terrifying banzai charge. Many Japanese survivors, too weak to fight, set off their own grenades, vowing to meet their comrades at the Yasakuni Shrine.

The end game near Buna was even more forbidding. After bleeding Australian and American units dry for three months, the Japanese outposts near Buna began to fall apart. In the last days scattered Japanese units made meaningless attacks, and scores of Japanese soldiers committed suicide. Few incidents during the Pacific War were more pitiful or more tragic than the end of the Japanese resistance on January 21, 1943. After withstanding heavy pressure from American and crack Australian infantry, a disintegrating Japanese battalion north of Buna was attacked by four companies of the U.S. 41st Division. Although attacked by a force no larger than those beaten off many times before, the Japanese perimeter, which at this time was deep inside Allied lines, simply fell apart. Allied artillery and mortars pounded the position in the morning. American infantry, without the aid of tanks, penetrated the perimeter quickly. Perhaps dazed by the bombardment or simply exhausted, Japanese infantry wandered in the open as American soldiers shot them down. In the words of one soldier, "We caught most of the Japs still underground or trying to extricate themselves from shattered bunkers. The garrison panicked and ran up Sanananda Road across our line of fire. We had great killing." At the end of the day the Americans counted 520 dead, one of the bloodiest days endured by the Japanese army up until that time. American losses were six killed. What made this incident so particularly wretched is that a large, well-garrisoned perimeter was exactly the type of position that could have arranged an orderly and relatively safe surrender. Fighting in a hopeless position, almost as many Japanese soldiers perished in that single spot in a few hours as the Americans had lost in the entire Buna campaign. Instead of honor the Japanese chose death. In doing so they taught yet another division that Japanese soldiers would not surrender and added fire to the lethal momentum already building.

The pattern seen first at Guadalcanal and Buna was repeated again and again in the Pacific War. The Allies would attack. The Japanese would fight with great courage and tactical skill, although not always with great strategic wisdom. American forces suffered painful losses, and most campaigns dragged on well past the date predicted by the U.S. commanders for victory. However, at some point, American firepower would begin to take its toll, and the Japanese resistance would begin to disintegrate into a macabre and senseless death orgy during which almost all victims were Japanese. So the tragedy at Buna was repeated often on a much-larger scale throughout the Pacific War. Among the most horrid examples were the Cliffs of Death on Saipan, the Meat Grinder on Iwo Jima, and the Suicide Caves on Okinawa.

As American troops on Guadalcanal learned firsthand that the Japanese would not surrender, they also learned a related and even more painful lesson: an attempt to surrender on the part of a Japanese soldier might actually be a ruse designed to enable the Japanese to take an American with him on his journey into death. The most dramatic such occurrence was an incident forgotten today but at the time known by every American soldier in the South Pacific—the infamous Goettge Patrol. Immediately after the American landing on Guadalcanal, a handful of Japanese and Korean construction laborers surrendered. One of the Japanese told the marines that others in his unit wanted to surrender. Lt. Col. Frank Goettge, the First Marine Division's intelligence officer, convinced commanding Gen. Vandegrift to allow him to take a twenty-five man patrol up the coast and arrange the surrender. Reluctantly, Vandegrift gave his permission, and the patrol left the next morning. By evening one survivor had made it back to American lines. It is very possible that the Goettge Patrol perished due to tactical incompetence and not Japanese design. However, to every marine it was a dramatic example that the Japanese were ruthless and treacherous. It was known to be difficult to get Japanese surrenders: from then on it was also believed to be dangerous. The outcome was that many American soldiers simply didn't try.

Dozens of veterans described small-scale versions of the Goettge Patrol that they witnessed in the Pacific. Lou Marvellous was a squad leader with the First Marine Division and gave interesting commentary on the fear and confusion caused by the Japanese.

> I have thought about the Japanese for fifty years. I had a high regard for Japanese soldiers. They were brave, tenacious, sly, and very good at pulling off the unexpected. But in another way, I feel that many of the things they did were simply stupid. They sacrificed their own men needlessly, for no purpose at all. During a battle along the Matanikau three or four were straggling toward us as though they were going to surrender. There must have been a dozen of us with a bead on them. Sure enough, one bent over and there was a carbine or submachine gun slung on his back that his comrade tried to grab. We shot them down instantly. Later we were out on a large operation. There were maybe a hundred of us. Suddenly, one Japanese officer comes charging out of the jungle screaming and waving his sword. We riddled him. What did he accomplish? He was only one man. What could he hope to accomplish? They did this type of thing so many times. It got to the point where we took no prisoners. It wasn't a written order but a way to survive. No one should take a chance to take a guy prisoner who might try to kill him.
>
> I don't know how you can defend this attitude. I feel the military in Japan fooled their people. Somehow they convinced their soldiers that their lives belonged to someone else. So the Japanese soldier was tough and smart, but at the end he was finished and could only blow himself up.

I have emphasized accounts of early engagements because they helped create a kind of battlefield culture in the Pacific. All of the events related above became lessons learned for soldiers trained later in the war. More important, each account was passed on from soldier to soldier. The rumor mill works overtime in war, and no doubt bogus or exaggerated accounts of Japanese treachery appeared in large numbers. As the war continued and more American soldiers received a good dose of political indoctrination and propaganda, the audience was well inclined to believe the worst of the stories. Sadly, as the war progressed, and the bloom of Japan's victories began to wane, it is very possible that more Imperial troops might have been willing to surrender had the situation allowed it. Unfortunately, these servants of the emperor met Americans increasingly convinced that the Japanese would not surrender, or if surrender was offered, it might prove a ruse. The Americans believed that it was not worth the risk to take prisoners. Japanese propaganda told soldiers and civilians alike that the Americans were butchers who would murder anyone tempted to capitulate. By 1944, to a sad degree, both sides were preaching a kind of truth.

Despite the vile circumstances, the American army made systematic efforts to take Japanese prisoners throughout the war. Each division had Japanese-American intelligence personnel who had, among their duties, the job of attempting to get Japanese soldiers to leave their entrenchments and surrender. In some cases they succeeded. Yet these men, despite brave work and a largely unheralded record, were swimming upstream against a powerful current of mutual bloodletting.

A tragedy took place in the South Pacific that stemmed largely from the grotesque manipulation of the Japanese people by Japan's military government. By successfully convincing their soldiers to find meaning in oblivion and to accept the frightening idea that spiritual purification comes through purposeful death, the Japanese government created the psychological framework for total war. I think that it is very possible that the well-earned image of Japan as a fanatical, even suicidal foe had a profound influence on the extremely brutal measures taken by the United States to end the Pacific War. In an era when the United States and other nations of the world may again be facing an enemy propounding a cult of death, this is a sobering thought.

PART 4

War and the Human Condition

Armageddon

An Interview with Max Hastings

C an there be anything new to say about the collapse of the Third Reich?
Sir Max Hastings, one of Great Britain's most respected military writers, convincingly shows that there is much more to the end of the Third
Reich than speculations about mystery weapons and accounts of those
murky final days in Hitler's Berlin bunker. Hastings's *Armageddon* (2004)
is an impressive and disturbing account of the defeat of Germany from
September 1944 to May 1945. This was nothing short of a cataclysm, and
Hastings recounts some of the "extraordinary things that happened to ordinary people" on both fronts. What emerges is a picture of suffering, degra-
dation, dignity, and profound moral complexity.

Hastings was an award-winning foreign correspondent for many years,
reporting from more than sixty countries for BBC TV and the *London
Evening Standard.* He has presented historical documentaries for BBC TV,
including in 2003 on Churchill and his generals. He has written eighteen
books on military history and current events, including *Bomber Command*
(which won the Somerset Maugham Prize for nonfiction), *The Battle for the
Falklands,* and *Overlord: D-Day and the Battle for Normandy.* He was editor
in chief of the *British Daily Telegraph* and *Evening Standard,* from which
he retired in 2002. Donald A. Yerxa, editor of *Historically Speaking,* interviewed Hastings in the Boston offices of the Historical Society on December 1, 2004.

DONALD A. YERXA: What drew you to the write an account of the battle
for Germany?

From Historically Speaking 6 (March/April 2005)

Sir Max Hastings: It was a bit of unfinished business. Twenty years ago, I wrote *Overload: D-Day and the Battle for Normandy,* which ended in September 1944. I have always had a nagging fascination with what happened afterward, in particular with why the Allies didn't win in 1944. At the beginning of September 1944, most of the Allied leadership, with the notable exception of Winston Churchill, was completely convinced that the war was going to be over by the end of the year. In the West, the Germans seemed completely beaten. The Western Allies had overwhelming superiority in tanks, aircraft, everything—you name it. So I wanted to look at this question of why we didn't end the war in 1944. Second, and almost as important, virtually all the books that have been written about this period look at either the Eastern or the Western front. And I wanted to set the two in context: to see what happened to the Western Allies in the context of what happened with the Soviets. This nearly overwhelmed me because it is such a huge subject. My wife, by the way, warned me not to write books that people can't hold up in bed. One has to remember that the last months of the Second World War witnessed the greatest human cataclysm of the twentieth century, and trying to cover all that ground did prove to be a big task. But, I must add, it became utterly fascinating.

Yerxa: Could you comment on your claims that the Germans and Russians in World War II were better warriors but worse human beings?

Hastings: This is a very important truth. When I wrote *Overlord,* I caused quite a lot of controversy by saying flatly that man for man, the German army was the best in the Second World War. This claim is generally accepted now, but when I first made it in 1984, it wasn't. British and American veterans took umbrage. When I was writing *Armageddon,* my assessment of the German army was confirmed. The evidence is so clear: again and again small numbers of Germans managed to hold up for hours, days, weeks much larger numbers of Allied soldiers. But I also realized that there was an important corollary: if we wanted British and American soldiers to fight like the Waffen–SS, they would have needed to become people like the Waffen–SS. And then, of course, the very values for which the whole war was fought would have been out the window. We have good grounds today to be enormously grateful that American and British veterans mostly preserved all the inhibitions and decencies of citizen-soldiers. In the main, these veterans never thought of themselves as warriors. They were bank clerks, laborers, train-drivers, and so on thrust into uniform to masquerade as warriors for a time. They wanted to do their duty and do it right, but equally they wanted to live to come home and share the fruits of victory. All this is very admirable, but of course you do pay a price because it takes much longer to win a war against German fanatics.

In the East, we had an ally who had nothing like the same concern for human life. Eisenhower, to provide an obvious example, was criticized for falling to reach Berlin in the last weeks of the war. I think he was absolutely right. Berlin was designated inside the Soviet zone. What would Eisenhower have said to the mothers and wives of American or British soldiers who had died to achieve a symbolic triumph? Joseph Stalin, Marshal Georgy Zhukov, and Marshal Ivan Konev were perfectly happy to see a hundred thousand Soviet soldiers die to achieve the great symbolic triumph of taking Berlin.

Having said all this, we have to be humble about the relative roles that the Western Allies had in the final defeat of the Germans. To be sure, the United States played an enormous part in providing the munitions and the transport that enabled the Soviets to reach Berlin as well as the British to keep fighting. But when one looks at the raw numbers, the Soviets paid the blood price. I don't mean that the war was a happy experience for British and American veterans; it was very terrible. But in ballpark terms, during the course of the war, American and British ground troops killed about two hundred thousand German soldiers, while the Russians killed about three and a half million. The United States, Britain, and France together lost about one million dead in the war. The Soviet Union lost twenty-seven million dead. Although we can be grateful that on the whole—with some notable question marks around strategic bombing—the Western Allies did preserve civilized values through the war, we needed the help of some very uncivilized people in order to bring down the Nazi tyranny. Had it not been for the Soviets who were prepared to lavish these huge quantities of blood, then an awful lot more American and British boys would have had to die to defeat Hitler.

Yerxa: Would you provide a very brief assessment of the military and strategic leadership of the Allies? Who stands out positively and negatively?

Hastings: The more I study military history, the more I come to the conclusion that the sort of people you need to win your wars are seldom if ever going to be ones you would call normal human beings. If you start with those people who win Congressional Medals of Honor or Victoria Crosses, many are regarded with deepest suspicion by other soldiers around them, who know they are made of weaker clay, and whose only ambition is not to win medals but to get home alive. I have been astounded to find how unpopular a lot of so-called heroes have been with those around them who have just been terrified by them. They have been awed by the qualities they have displayed but do not want to have any part of it themselves.

Now if you look at the command level, a significant number of great generals have verged on being unhinged. If you read Zhukov's memoirs, he sounds quite rational, and you might be fooled into thinking he was a normal human being. But there is not a shred of evidence that the Soviet generals were anything but brutes. Only brutes could have prospered in Stalin's universe of blood. While Zhukov was probably the most effective Allied commander in the Second World War, his effectiveness was a function of his absolute ruthless treatment of his own men, never mind the enemy. Zhukov handled huge forces, millions of men, with a confidence that few, if any, Allied commanders could match. He drove forward in Operation Bagration, the Russian campaign of the summer of 1944 that Williamson Murray has called the greatest ground operation of the war. Soviet commanders handled their armies with much more panache and aplomb than the Western Allies in the last year of the war. But they also did so with an absolute indifference to losses. To provide one striking example, one need only refer to the Soviet invasion of Romania, which the Russians considered one of the easiest operations of their war. The Romanian army collapsed, the Germans retreated rapidly, and the Red Army took Romania in a fortnight. The Soviets lost more people in the Romania operation alone than the British and Canadian armies did in the entire northwest Europe campaign.

George Patton, commander of U.S. 3rd Army, was undoubtedly the most imaginative American commander in Europe. It is a pity that he wasn't either holding down Omar Bradley's job as commander of the 12th Army Group or in charge of Courtney Hodges's 1st Army, because there was never any chance that the 3rd Army's southern axis was going to be the line of advance into Germany. Patton's sense of driving urgency might have got the Allies into Germany faster. But given his behavior in the famous "slapping incidents" in Sicily—when on two occasions he slapped men claiming combat fatigue and called them out as cowards—there was no chance he would get to lead the primary drive into Germany. Moreover, Patton was hopeless in dealing with allies. With his absolute contempt for Field Marshal Sir Bernard Montgomery and hatred of the Brits, it would have been very difficult to put Patton in any role where he would have to work closely with them. So it was probably inevitable that Patton was relegated to a subordinate role, but I think the conventional wisdom that he was a great pursuit commander is correct. Although it must be mentioned, that in the hard, close fighting there was not much evidence that Patton could get a better performance out of his people than any other American commander. He, too, was faced with the limitations of citizen armies. General Hodges was a pretty pathetic figure. He shouldn't have been commanding an army in Europe. General Jacob "Jake" Devers, head of the U.S. 6th Army Group in southern France, was a more impressive commander than either Hodges or Bradley.

Montgomery, like Patton, possessed an uncongenial personality and was somewhat unhinged. How could you be such an intelligent man, as he undoubtedly was, and believe as late as 1944 that the Americans had no idea how to make war and that he should be in charge of all American forces? By this stage, not many Americans would have said they were better soldiers than the Brits, but they had certainly seen nothing in the British performance to suggest that the British were better than they were.

Eisenhower has been so much criticized. It is true he wasn't a very great battlefield commander. But he displayed tremendous ability in holding together the alliance through to 1945, when by that stage the British and the Americans were almost sick of the sight of each other. We hear this line nowadays in Iraq that the British and Americans are natural allies, but all alliances are difficult. And in the Second World War, the British and the Americans found it very difficult to work together. To this day, the British are haunted by a nagging sense that we think we ran the world better than the United States does. And sometimes we are stupid enough to let it show. Americans, in turn, sometimes claim that the British are rather plodding and pompous. So it did require the genius that Eisenhower displayed to keep these people speaking to each other.

YERXA: What about the German military leadership?

HASTINGS: It is ironic that all the German generals complained after the war how impossible it was to work with Hitler. Several remarked that it was a tragedy that the Western Allies didn't reach Berlin before the Russians. Yet if the German generals had done exactly what Hitler had ordered them to do, the war would have been over a lot sooner. They couldn't help themselves from trying to frustrate some of Hitler's mad ideas. Until the very end they used their best professional skills in the West as well as the East. But despite their skill as soldiers, the German generals deserve the contempt of history for their failure to act effectively against Hitler. The bomb plot of July 1944 was pretty feeble. When I asked middle-ranking officers in 2002 why they fought on to the bitter end, some responded that they had sworn an oath. They still felt that their oath to Hitler had some validity. Very commonly they also would say that they had to keep the Russians out of Germany. That may be so, but why try to thwart the Western Allies? It only made sense to fight to the end in the East if you were going to help the Americans and Brits enter Germany. They have no good answer for this. I have been very impressed with a journal I discovered in my research kept by a Danish journalist, Paul von Stemann, who spent the war in Berlin. He made a lot of interesting reflections about German behavior in the last stages of the war. Stemann noted that in the last year the German people lapsed into an almost catatonic state. They seemed morally and physically paralyzed, incapable of any constructive action to avert this great steamroller of fate that was bearing down upon them. It is such a puzzle to account for how this extraordinary paralysis was matched by a willingness to keep fighting.

YERXA: Did the memory of 1918 play into this?

HASTINGS: Actually, there was a terrific concern on the Allied side about not repeating 1918. One of the most interesting marginal issues at the end of the war concerned the decision to conceal to the world the extent to which the Allies had broken the German signals traffic, the Ultra business. They obviously didn't want everyone to know how successful the British and Americans had been at code breaking. There was a subplot to this. The British did not want the Germans to know that their codes had been broken, because they did not want to give German generals the excuse to say what they had said in 1918: they hadn't been fairly beaten—there had been a stab in the back. Certainly Churchill and others were very anxious that the German people have absolutely squarely in their minds the fact that they had been beaten.

YERXA: Would you speak a bit more to the tensions between the Americans and the British in the last stages of the war?

HASTINGS: There was the feeling among the Brits that it was terribly unfair that they had suffered so much since 1939 and were so weary and were still being hit by rockets, and here were all these rich, healthy, clean, young Americans pouring off the ships to claim the rewards of victory from the Old World without, as the Old World saw it, having borne their share of the Old World's pain. Most Brits were either openly or secretly bitter because they felt their nation had been pushed to the side of the stage. Churchill thought this more than anyone. By 1945 he was very sore with Roosevelt. He felt that FDR failed to understand the menace of the Soviets, and he was weary of Roosevelt's insults at the Allied summits where he made it clear that he was more interested in talking with Stalin than Churchill. I agree with Roy Jenkins that while Churchill pleaded logistical reasons for not attending Roosevelt's funeral, by that stage he had no appetite to attend. Churchill believed that FDR had let them all down since he was the only one with the power to exercise some restraining influence on Stalin. Maybe Roosevelt couldn't have done it, but he didn't even try. And Churchill was pretty sore about that.

YERXA: One of your major arguments is that English and American writers tend to downplay the extent to which Allied victory in 1945 depended upon the ability of Stalin's armies to accept a level of human sacrifice necessary to defeat Hitler. Further, you argue that the Allied victory was morally compromised by this dependence upon Stalin, who was as much a monster as Hitler. Was there any "good" alternative available to the Western Allies? Realistically speaking, could unspeakable tragedy have been averted?

HASTINGS: There were some, including the head of the British army, who disliked the Russians so much that they would have preferred to have been beaten on their own in 1941 than to enter into any relationship with the Soviets. I'm not making a serious suggestion of this kind, but the fact was that even with the United States in the war, the vast might of the Red Army was needed. Without the Russians, we would have beaten Hitler in the end, but it would have been a terrible process that would have cost an awful lot more British and American lives. All I am really suggesting is that we should be more willing to acknowledge the moral price we paid. Eisenhower could justly call his memoirs *Crusade in Europe* because the Western Allies had indeed been fighting with remarkable unselfishness for the freedom of Europe. But in order to destroy the Nazi tyranny, we did ally ourselves with an equally evil tyranny.

I'm not saying that we shouldn't have had anything to do with the Russians. But I am saying that before we get too pleased with ourselves about the great achievement of the democracies in the Second World War, we ought to recognize what a dirty business it became to have to throw away Poland, Romania, Czechoslovakia, and all the other Eastern European countries as the Soviets' blood price. Churchill was obliged in the end to recognize that having entered the war in the hope of freeing the whole of Europe, he had to settle for freeing half of it, sacrificing the other half to the Soviets. Churchill felt so savage about the loss of Eastern Europe in 1945 that he seemed to be willing to consider anything to save the Poles. But the blunt truth—as FDR perceived—was that the only way to deny the Soviets their conquests in Eastern Europe was by fighting them. Virtually no one in either the United States or Great Britain had any appetite for a war against the Soviets. In this sense, Roosevelt was entitled to say that he was the realist and Churchill was the fantasist in not being prepared to face this reality squarely.

YERXA: What is your reaction to the phrase "the good war"?

HASTINGS: Insofar as any war is a good war, the Second World War was a good war because we can say unquestionably that Nazism was an appalling evil. If one wants to take an optimistic view, what we can say is that World

War II did not finally achieve its objectives until the late 1980s when the veterans had their real reward with the collapse of the Soviet tyranny belatedly in the wake of the Nazi tyranny. So one can reasonably argue that the true end of the war was the late 1980s.

YERXA: You make a compelling case for the moral complexity of the end of the war in Europe. Have military writers tended to embrace a simplistic view of World War II as a triumphalist crusade?

HASTINGS: There are two types of military history. One is what one might call romantic military history. I was talking to the military historian Russell Weigley shortly before he died about a very well-known historian who had a lot of success writing books about the American fighting man. Weigley said that he was sad to see a respected historian raising monuments rather than writing history. In the same breath, Weigley noted that a veteran told him that these books made him feel good about himself. A huge amount of it is produced, and it sells very well. There is nothing wrong with this romantic military history as long as we recognize its limitations. It is a celebration. This is not just an American phenomenon. Every year in Britain we celebrate the Battle of Britain without asking many hard questions in our media about its limitations. The Battle of Britain was a success within certain limits. The bald truth is that if Hitler hadn't invaded the Soviet Union, he could have come back in 1941 and invaded Britain. Having said that, I take an intensely romantic view of veterans. I always feel privileged to talk to people who experienced things beyond anything I have encountered in my own life. But we must also ask the hard questions. We should not be surprised that many people in their eighties who have lived through this era want to imbue what happened to them with a romantic aura. God knows, I would if I'd been through what they've been through.

Romantic military history, then, clearly has limitations. For example, in any given battle about one quarter of the men who were fighting would lose their bowels in their trousers. These are the things that romantic historians don't care to dwell on, but it is just one of the sordid realities that you try to come to terms with. And, of course, there are military histories that attempt to analyze what happened. The first generation of people who wrote military history after the Second World War didn't write too much about the nitty-gritty because they were writing for people who had been there and knew it all. They knew what a Sherman tank did, what a Flying Fortress was like. But now my generation is writing for a lot of people who do not know these things. So I try to explain things like how battles were fought and how armor and infantry worked together. I include a very good line in the book from an

American officer: "A few men carry your attack, and all the rest sort of turn up at the objective later." This is a profound truth. You cannot expect more than a small minority in a unit to be real fighters. The rest are not cowards, but they certainly aren't as brave as those few. This is true of all armies. So this other kind of nonromantic military history needs to pick things like this apart and analyze them for the benefit of people who, thank God, have never had to be on a battlefield. When I write a book, of course, I think about what will sell, but I also ask myself, "What can I tell people that they don't know already?" So in this book, for example, I say virtually nothing about Hitler in the bunker. We've been over all that. Far better to talk about aspects of this part of the war that people haven't thought much about.

YERXA: What about the other side of this coin? What about those writers who are also unwilling to embrace moral complexities not because of celebratory sentiments but because they want war to yield to higher, almost purist moral standards?

HASTINGS: I don't buy such arguments at all. Of course, no war is morally perfect. One of the worst diseases of our time is the notion that we must pursue moral absolutes. Most of life is about making very difficult marginal choices about morality. It is never going to be 100 percent, and that's why we should always exhibit some sympathy for our rulers when they make decisions about peace or war. I happen to be a critic of the Iraq business. There well might be a case to be made for using force against the North Koreans, Iranians, or someone else who threatens the peace of the world with weapons of mass destruction. What caused some of us to say before the Iraq war began that we were skeptical about going in was that we were fearful that it would compromise the case for using force in a better cause. So it is madness, I think, to say that nothing is worth the use of force. When civilized societies lose the strength of purpose to be prepared to use force for relatively good causes, we might as well all give up because we've had it. We must have the confidence to make these decisions, but obviously every time we use force in a cause that is not very good, it weakens our ability to muster the will of our society to use force in a better cause. In the current situation, a lot of us are very worried about what the Iranians are doing with their nuclear capability. And we do feel pretty sore toward Bush, Cheney, and Rumsfeld because we feel they have made it harder to use force on something that looks as if it may really matter.

YERXA: What would you like the reader to take away from the book?

HASTINGS: Although I write military history, above all I am interested in what happened as human experience. And if I were asked to give one good reason to read my book, it would be that we have stupid people who don't know any history saying today that we live in a terrible world: 9/11, al Qaeda, and so on. It bears saying again and again that we are an incredibly privileged and pampered generation. One need only spend five minutes considering the experiences of what people went through in the Second World War as a whole—especially in the final cataclysmic phase when more than one hundred million people were, as I say in my book, "locked in bloody embrace"— to conclude that we are so very fortunate today. I am always fascinated listening to people describing what happened. Tom Brokaw called these people "the greatest generation." I'd phrase it a bit differently: it was the generation to whom the greatest things happened. One never ceases to be amazed by the summits of courage that some men achieved and the depths of baseness that others plumbed. I do believe that in order to set our own experience in proper context, we need to understand what happened to them.

I would especially hope that the message of humility comes through. The only case for writing books of this kind is to teach a new generation something about what happened to a previous generation. Every time I write a book like this, I listen hour after hour to the experiences of hundreds of men and women who have endured things mostly far beyond our experience. And I always come away from listening to them having learned something. I was especially moved by the story of Michael Wieck, an East Prussian Jew who suffered terribly under the Nazis and miraculously survived to welcome the Red Army as his deliverers when they stormed Königsberg in April 1945. The Russians didn't give a damn for the yellow stars on his family's sleeves. They regarded them as Germans. He ended up in a Russian concentration camp where he had ghastly, unspeakable experiences. He eventually escaped to the West in 1947 when he was seventeen years old. And after I listened to his terrible experiences for three or four hours, I remarked that he must have felt his childhood was stolen from him. "No, I don't feel that at all," he said. "I've met so many people who have so-called normal childhoods but whose lives have been completely screwed up. In my case, since 1947 I have had a wonderful life. My childhood was different from other people's childhoods, but you won't hear me say that it was somehow stolen from me. I feel no ill will of any kind toward either the Russians or the Germans." I was profoundly moved by such generosity of spirit from a person who had suffered so much.

It is always about humility, about being so grateful for what we have, and also about being hugely impressed by the dignity and generosity of spirit with which many people have endured far worse things than we will ever have to. I write less and less in my books about which division went where and so on, because I really don't think that matters much unless you are writing for West Point or Sandhurst. What humans did and what happened to them is what really counts, and what really matters is trying to teach ourselves something about how previous generations have behaved that might help us to behave, if not better, at least a little less badly.

The War of the World

An Interview with Niall Ferguson

Niall Ferguson is one of the world's best-known historians. In 2004 *Time* magazine named him as one of the world's hundred most-influential people. He is author of several books that advance bold, often controversial theses, including *The Pity of War: Explaining World War One* (1998), *Empire: The Rise and Demise of the British World Order and the Lessons for Global Power* (2003), and *Colossus: The Rise and Fall of the American Empire* (2004). His latest book, *The War of the World: Twentieth-Century Conflict and the Decline of the West* (2006), is an extended essay on why the twentieth century was the bloodiest in history. On September 13, 2006, *Historically Speaking* editor Donald A. Yerxa caught up with Ferguson at his Harvard office.

DONALD A. YERXA: What is your basic argument in *The War of the World*?
NIALL FERGUSON: *The War of the World* asks the question, "Why was the twentieth century so violent when it was in so many ways a century of unprecedented progress in economic, scientific, and political terms?" I felt when I asked this question that the conventional answers were not very compelling because they didn't tell you where and when specifically the violence happened. And I thought if I could answer that question—why were some places and some periods so excessively violent—I might actually make a contribution. *The War of the World* says that places that were ethnically very mixed, that experienced economic volatility, and that were located on a sort of imperial fault line were likely to experience extreme violence in the twentieth century. And that's why Central and Eastern Europe, North Korea, and Manchuria were very dangerous places, and Canada wasn't.

From Historically Speaking 8 (November/December 2006)

YERXA: You state in the book that "When a multiethnic empire mutated into a nation state, the result could only be carnage." Do the circumstances of ethnic disintegration, economic volatility, and empires in decline necessarily unleash the basest instincts of ordinary people in "tribal bloodletting"?

FERGUSON: The problem is that the ideal of the nation-state implies homogeneity, that everybody in France is a Frenchman. And it's very hard to apply that model the further east you go in Europe because the patchwork of linguistic, ethnic, and religious settlement is just too great. To create a nation-state called Turkey out of what was left of the Ottoman Empire at the end of the First World War was almost by definition going to lead to conflicts. The Armenians, who were Christians and who were seen as being close to Russia geographically and politically, were in some ways the first victims of a succession of genocidal conflicts that arose when empires tried to become nation-states. In that sense carnage was likely. Of course, carnage took different forms. At the "starter" level it consisted of merely expelling people or discriminating against them, treating them as second-class citizens. It didn't mean automatically that genocidal policies would arrive. War was necessary for the process of homogenization to take on an extremely violent, genocidal form. I'm not sure how else the circle can be squared in multiethnic societies other than through fragmentation. Balkanization is the essence of the alternative scenario where the empire simply breaks apart into multiple mini-nation-states, which was the Austro-Hungarian "solution," if that's the right word.

YERXA: The U.K. edition of *The War of the World* carries the subtitle *History's Age of Hatred,* whereas the U.S. edition's subtitle is *Twentieth-Century Conflict and the Descent of the West.* Which captures your argument better?

FERGUSON: Well, I like them both. In a way *History's Age of Hatred* is a snappier title. British subtitles tend to be shorter. Hatred is at the center of the book. One of the big questions that I'm asking is, "What makes hatred happen?" Hatred so great that it can lead to millions of deaths is a pretty important thing to understand, and I did feel when I embarked on this project that there was a weakness in our historical understanding of hatred. When historians use phrases like "ancient hatred" or "deep-rooted anti-Semitism," they leave a lot of questions unanswered. And the central paradox of the book is that the countries that produced some of the most violent ethnic conflict had also experienced very high levels of integration and assimilation. So there seems to be a very complex relation between hatred and love that the book is talking about. But the book is also about the *Descent of the West.* A central argument that I want to make is that we can't understand the twentieth century as a Western century, as a Western triumph, or as an American century. The year 1900 was the zenith of Western power, and from then on it was a very bumpy road downhill. I think that's one of the more interesting arguments in the book. So I suppose I'm rather torn. In a sense the book needs at least two subtitles and possibly more. Maybe I tried to put too much in between one set of hard covers.

YERXA: I read somewhere that you call the book the "Everest of my career." Is *The War of the World* in some way the culmination of your earlier work?

FERGUSON: I wasn't implying that it is a mountainous achievement in itself, but it felt like scaling Everest. I tried to write a book that took in WWII and the Holocaust and to set those events in the broader context of conflicts. It's the culmination of, I'd say, twenty years of thinking about these issues and teaching these subjects, trying to come up with a sort of a unified-field theory of the twentieth century. It is, of course, a fool's enterprise. But that was the idea. And I guess it's up to readers and reviewers whether I'm one of those climbers who gets to the top of Everest and plants a flag or one of the ones you find half-frozen somewhere on the lower foothills. I don't think I got to the summit. I'm not satisfied with it. I'm never satisfied with any book. But it was worth a try because I felt as if at some point I had to reckon with particularly the period up until 1945. And having done that, I feel in some measure liberated from it.

YERXA: Where do you go from Everest?

FERGUSON: Forward in time and to the level of the individual in focus. *The War of the World* is a macrohistory. It attempts to embrace the movements of millions. The next two books I want to write will be biographies. Both will be set largely in the post-1945 world. One is going to be a biography of Siegmund Warburg, who was in many ways the most influential financial figure—at least in Britain—after 1945. The other will be a biography of Henry Kissinger, which is an Everest—or should I say K2?—of another sort. So that will represent a decisive break in style of history and in period.

YERXA: What are some of the ways the twentieth century makes more sense using your framework?

FERGUSON: I've already mentioned the point that the descent of the West is a useful conceptual framework. Suddenly you're less surprised about what is happening in China if you understand it as the culmination of a process dating back to 1904, if not earlier, in Japan. Interestingly, the cold war made a lot more sense to me when I recast it as the Third World War, sort of a relocation of conflict to new regions once the great Eurasian war zones had been partitioned. And I thought that was a very useful insight, that the war zones of the world from 1904 to 1953 were East-Central Europe and

Korea-Manchuria. By 1953 that was over. You couldn't have a war there any more because if you did, the entire world would be blown up. And that's why you ended up with Guatemala, Cambodia, Angola, and so forth as the new war zones on the periphery. Economic volatility is a concept that historians don't use much. I think this book shows how useful it is in identifying the 1920s, 1930s, and 1940s as the danger decades and also explaining why our time seems so very smooth, at least in the West. It's a far less volatile time economically, and when volatility goes down, the stakes go down in terms of social conflict.

YERXA: In a recent review of your book, Paul Johnson argues that you don't pay sufficient attention to the connection between secularization and genocide and slaughter—that "humanity even with religious restraints is a force for horror as well as progress. Without them, its turpitude knows no bounds." Do you see any connection?

FERGUSON: I haven't seen that review. But I argue early on that there is a limit to how much we can explain extreme violence with reference to religion or indeed with reference to the pseudo-religions of political ideology, such as, extreme socialism or extreme nationalism, that came into existence in the nineteenth century. The extreme ideologies of nationalism and communism are ubiquitous; so are the monotheistic ideologies of Christianity, Islam, and Judaism. They're there, everywhere, available before 1900. And that makes it very hard to answer my questions, "Why there, and then specifically? Why was Ukraine/Poland so much more violent than, say, Sweden?" I think that's the best answer I can give to you. I do not mean to undervalue the importance of secularization and particularly not to understate the role of atheism in some of the most unspeakable regimes in the twentieth century. Both the Soviet Union and Mao's China were hell-bent—and that's perhaps the best phrase—on replacing traditional religion with their own secular religion. And that had terrible consequences. But I don't see that as a very good answer to the question of why extreme violence occurred where it did and when it did. Of course, when you talk about ethnic conflict, you are in some measures talking about religion, because ethnicity is about language, it's about culture, it's about religion. Ostensibly, Armenians had been slaughtered for their religion in 1915; ostensibly, Bosnian Muslims were being slaughtered for their religion in the 1990s. But on close inspection those were not wars of religion. They were ethnic conflicts. And the communities were being targeted for more than just their doctrinal religious beliefs. Finally I think it's worth saying that another historian is exploring this line of inquiry already and very successfully, namely Michael Burleigh, who wrote *Earthly Powers: Religion and Politics from the French Revolution to the Great War* (2005) and whose *Sacred Causes: Religion and Politics from the European Dictators to Al Qaeda* (2006) has just come out. And the latter is really the book that Paul Johnson is looking for. So I didn't see any point in retracing Burleigh's steps. I hugely respect his work, as I respect Paul Johnson's work, but my contribution is different. And I suppose I do think it offers a better answer to the big question of what causes megadeath.

YERXA: Based on your work, is there any reason to think that humans can be altruistic and not filled with hatred?

FERGUSON: The key thing to remember is that one in twenty-two deaths in the twentieth century was violent, and twenty-one in twenty-two were natural. In that sense, the norm is still peace. It's not the norm for human beings to engage in hatred and to commit hate crimes, war crimes. That's still abnormal behavior, even in the twentieth century. It's clear that the way in which the human society works is predicated on our being able to cooperate and build bonds of trust beyond our immediate kinship group. Otherwise, there would be no civilization; there would only be Hobbes's war of all against all. And in a sense what interests me about the twentieth century is the extent to which there is a spectacular breakdown of quite sophisticated civilizations. After all, Germany as a civilization really was state of the art in the 1920s in so many ways. Its descent into barbarism is a spectacular occurrence. And there were Germans behaving altruistically in the midst of all that mayhem despite all the incentives being in the other direction. I don't think my view of human nature is excessively pessimistic. I am really concerned in this book with the aberrant behavior that we should all try to avoid in the future. That is part of the point of the book: let's try to understand what causes really large-scale conflicts. I still sense that we're still quite a long way from understanding this. Since such horrific violence does represent a dramatic break with what might be called our normal human impulses and is at odds with what is central to civilization, we have to explain it.

YERXA: How has the channel 4 series based on the book been received in the United Kingdom?

FERGUSON: Getting people in early summer to watch six films about mass death was asking a lot, especially with the World Cup going on. You had to choose between the war of the world and the cup of the world, which is the joke I made at the time. The ratings were extremely good. We had somewhere in the region of two million viewers at the peak, and that's a big percentage of the UK audience, something like one in ten viewers. So I was very happy about that. As with all projects that attempt to challenge received wisdom, there was something less than unanimous assent. But the debate that happened was reasonably dignified. The series was very beautifully filmed and tremendously well executed. It went down well particularly with those people who don't read history books. And the reason I do television is that you can never get two million people to read a book like this. But you can get them to watch six hours of television. In a really magic moment a bus driver said to me, "Oh, I watched your program last night, and I never knew anything about all that. It was absolutely fascinating." And I thought, well, that's the point of doing it.

YERXA: How do you approach writing a book that is also the companion to a major television series?

FERGUSON: Both *Empire* and *War of the Worlds* were written first as scripts, then as books. When you write a script or a series of scripts, they go through many drafts, and there is a lot of teamwork involved in honing the argument. Having a good bombproof argument is the essence of getting it right in television. Of course, once you strip out the directions, what you're left with is a very pathetic thing, barely an op-ed. But although it's a very small and pathetic thing, its structure is very strong. Then the task is to flesh it out, to add all the beautiful detail that television doesn't leave room for. That can be very satisfying, provided you've kept all your research materials in good order and provided there's a decent amount of time between finishing the scripts and delivering the book. Unfortunately you never do, and there never is.

YERXA: In a recent *Foreign Affairs* essay, "The Next War of the World," you extend your argument to the twenty-first century, maintaining that the Middle East manifests some of the same characteristics responsible for the worst violence of the twentieth century. Is there an alternative to a drift toward chaos and a repeat of the past century's slaughter?

FERGUSON: Well, I hope so. The thing that's really disturbing is that the processes that I am describing—this toxic mix of ethnic conflict, economic volatility, and imperial decline—are quite hard to reverse. I am pessimistic about the Middle East. The forces at work there are extraordinarily potent, and it's not clear to me that an irenic policy formulated by the international community can prevent the escalation of violence between Sunni and Shia. Of course, it is possible for multiethnic societies to avoid plunging into the abyss. All they need, in crude Fergusonian terms, is to avoid economic volatility and to have a sort of strategic neutrality imposed upon them. It's not inconceivable that that could happen. There is a possible future in which economic stabilization is achieved, and there isn't a conflict between the U.S. and Iran. It's just that the possibility of that future seems quite small. It's going to be hard to get there. And part of the point of writing the book and particularly the *Foreign Affairs* article is to say, "Look, this is the problem. It is really, really serious. If you think you've seen violence in the Middle East, you ain't seen nothing yet." It could get much, much nastier than it has; therefore, we have a very urgent political responsibility to try to avoid that kind of repetition.

YERXA: Is preemptive military action against Iran likely?

FERGUSON: Well, the problem is that half of the *War of the World* is a quite detailed critique of appeasement. Nineteen thirty-eight would have been a great time to stop the Third Reich in its tracks. Nineteen thirty-nine was too late. There's nothing worse than making crude parallels between the 1930s and any subsequent events. That was Eden's mistake in the Suez and everybody's mistake in Vietnam. I would be the last person to simply say that Ahmadinejad is Hitler. That would be very silly. But I do think that we need to take seriously the proposition that with nuclear weapons, Iran will be in a position to dictate terms throughout the region, including to Israel. And we need to recognize the unlikelihood that Israel will simply submit to its own liquidation. There are forms of preemption that have much lower costs than appeasement. And the critical point is that appeasement ended up having disastrously high costs. It may well be that there are ways other than warfare to draw the sting out of this particular venomous beast. But the probability is quite low that this can achieved by peaceful means.

YERXA: Is talk of a long war against radical Islam inflated?

FERGUSON: Well in some ways, I'm sympathetic to the view that radical Islam is as much of an internationally subversive ideology as communism ever was. I don't buy the idea that there is an Islamo-fascism, or whatever you care to call it, because I don't think it has much to do with fascism at all. But it does resemble bolshevism in the sense that it aims for an international revolution. The question is whether it makes sense to wage cold war while Islamo-bolshevik organizations have very limited power. It would be a different story if bin Laden disposed of the oil revenues of Saudi Arabia, but right now, it is a skeletal, fragmented organization. And it's not actually responsible for anything like as much violence right now as conflicts within Islam between Sunnis and Shiites. I respect Huntington's clash of civilizations thesis, but most of the violence that has happened since 1993 has been within his civilizations, not between them. And I think we should be more worried about war within Islam than war against it, frankly. War within Islam could really blow the Middle East up more than any clash of civilizations.

YERXA: ABC News recently put out a piece on your connections to the John McCain camp. Would you care to comment on that?

FERGUSON: I've met John McCain and been impressed by him. He's a very well-read man. But to suggest that I'm advising him or am part of his kitchen cabinet is to exaggerate my significance by several orders of magnitude. I don't have any pretensions to be so grand, and I'm sure he has found more reliable and experienced people to be advised by than me.

YERXA: What do you see as the public role of the historian?

FERGUSON: We don't have anything to go on other than history when we're trying to address questions like the ones we're discussing here. What causes conflict? How can it be avoided, if at all? And if historians don't attempt to address these questions in a public way, then someone else will do it. I never really understand why anybody criticizes me for attempting to reach a mass audience or addressing questions of contemporary import. It seems strange to me that one should be castigated for reaching out to people not privileged enough to go to Harvard. If I just sat at Harvard and educated the people who are smart enough and lucky enough to get here, I would presumably be accused of elitism. But when I attempt to offer historical insight to people who drive buses, that's not good either. I don't quite don't know how one gets this right. The problem is that if you express opinions that are seen as being on the right side of the ideological spectrum in the academy, you are much more likely to draw fire. Apparently it is permissible to be a public intellectual on the left, but if you express sentiments to the right of Noam Chomsky, you are in for trouble.

YERXA: You are both a scholar and a public intellectual. Which role do you relish the most? Or do you not make such a distinction?

FERGUSON: That distinction doesn't really exist. What I do as a scholar can be published in different formats and at different lengths with varying numbers of footnotes. But I don't think that there is a fundamental difference in the quality of the underlying ideas. I read as much as I can, think as much as I can, and then to try to articulate what insights I have had in the various formats and media that seem to work. That can be a journal article, but it can also be an op-ed in the *Los Angeles Times*. Actually, the ideas that began in a journal article often end up in an op-ed. There is a process of distillation. There is also a process of simplification. But it remains the case, even at the stage when you're working on a PhD, that if you can't sum it up in two sentences, then there is probably something wrong with it.

YERXA: You seem to have been the inspiration for the Irwin character in Alan Bennett's play *The History Boys*. One journalist has described Irwin as "an amoral TV historian turned amoral political aide, famed for his willingness to argue the unthinkable." How does all this feel to you? Is it par for the course when you become a very visible public intellectual?

FERGUSON: When I went to see the play, I never expected it to be remotely about me. Alan Bennett is one of my favorite heroes. I never considered myself remotely interesting enough to be a target for his satirical pen. So I went to the play not really expecting to be in it, and there it was. There's this scene in the play where my *Pity of War* is very explicitly spoofed, and Bennett says in the notes to the published version of the play that Irwin is partly based on me. [*laughing*] My first reaction was to want a stiff drink. My second was to be faintly flattered, and my third was to think, "Okay, why is it wrong for Irwin to encourage his pupils to think against the current and challenge the conventional wisdom?" *The History Boys* is a funny skit, but it does two things with which I take issue insofar as one should take issue with such things. It understates the importance of dialectical thinking in history. Irwin is doing his job very well in fact. He's getting the boys to think against the current, and he gets them into Oxford. I benefited from that experience, and so did Alan Bennett. Another problem is that it quite deliberately aligns Irwin, the contrarian television historian, with the spin doctors of New Labour. But hang on a second. There's an ideological bait and switch there. It wasn't the television dons who became the spin doctors. None of Labour's spin doctors originated in the academy. So there's a cheap elision there, and it allows the British audience to equate in its mind the television dons and the spin doctors. But actually these are separate beasts. Oddly enough somebody who had seen the play in New York gave me a very American response. She said that it was obvious that Irwin was the good teacher. And she told me with a completely straight face how much she liked the play, which for her revealed how a good teacher should go about his business. I was reassured by that. It made me feel that I had made the right move by coming to the States.

Afterword

Military History Today

Jeremy Black

A mong military historians there is a general tendency to decry the state of the profession and to argue that the subject is overly neglected and actively shunned. Certainly, compared to what was taught in the past, there has been a decline—in favor of social history—of such staples as constitutional, diplomatic, legal, and military history. Within this span, it is reasonable to complain of the neglect of the last, not least in job searches, but only if this more general situation is understood. Furthermore, military history has the great advantage of having an additional basis in the service academies. There the approach is generally utilitarian but, particularly in the United States and to a lesser extent Britain, this does not preclude high academic standards. Moreover, if military historians feel under threat, it is worth noting that malaise is the condition of scholars: almost everyone feels underappreciated, even gender historians who have benefited greatly from developments in recent decades.

It is also necessary to note differences among military historians. The operational historians (sometimes unfairly but frequently all too accurately referred to in terms of drum-and-trumpet history) are indeed neglected within the academy. Yet those looking at wider dimensions, such as, the staples of war and society and war and the state, are generally assured of an audience. Indeed, the "history" in these cases is as much explored by sociologists, anthropologists, and political scientists as by those seen more conventionally as historians. In part, therefore, the discussion of military history today is a case of tensions among military historians about the character of military history. This debate is not always explicit but in practice exists not simply in terms of the content of the subject but also in terms of the way in which topics are pursued and presented as well as of the powerful issues of patronage and appointment and publication strategies. These latter issues are difficult to discuss. It is easier to probe questions about the appropriateness of the standard approach to military history. This approach is characterized by a fascination with technology as a definition of capability and an explanation of change and by a focus on the Western way of war. The West dominates attention not simply because it is indeed important, but because it is seen as setting global standards for effectiveness. This is an aspect of a tendency to dismiss non-Western military history as primitive.

These fundamental parameters of the subject are, in turn, linked to other issues. The fascination with technology and, more generally, with the material culture of war contributes to a presentation of military history in terms of revolutionary developments rather than of incrementalism, understood in terms of an evolutionary change based on trial and error. This is mistaken, as incrementalism is crucial, not least in terms of the response to allegedly revolutionary developments. The latter have to be grasped, a response defined, and the response embedded in terms of procurement and training. These responses involve what may be seen as cultural dimensions, and these repay attention in a subject that is frequently overly oriented toward battle, whether operational or in terms of the experience of war. A response open to cultural dimensions is also less overly determined, not least in terms of the habitual emphasis on the material aspects of war.

Allowing for these contrasting approaches, military history is worth studying not only for the light it throws on war past, present, and future but also because of the centrality of this history to much else in the past, not only political developments but also social and cultural counterparts.

Further Readings

The literature on military history is, of course, vast. The following titles represent some of the most important recent scholarly contributions (along with a few modern classics) to the historiographical themes highlighted in this volume: the current state of academic military history, military revolutions, the future of war, and soldiering, along with the related issues of war and culture and military thought. Additional recent titles dealing with other aspects of military history not discussed in this volume (naval history and thought, air power, and war in global perspective) are also included.

Military Revolution

Boot, Max. *War Made New: Technology, Warfare, and the Course of History, 1500 to Today.* New York: Gotham Books, 2006.

Downing, Brian M. *The Military Revolution and Political Change: Origins of Democracy and Autocracy in Early Modern Europe.* Princeton: Princeton University Press, 1992.

Knox, MacGregor, and Williamson Murray, eds. *The Dynamics of Military Revolution, 1300–2050.* Cambridge: Cambridge University Press, 2001.

Parker, Geoffrey. *The Military Revolution: Military Innovation and the Rise of the West, 1500–1800.* 2nd ed. Cambridge: Cambridge University Press, 1996.

Rogers, Clifford J., ed. *The Military Revolution Debate: Readings on the Military Transformation of Early Modern Europe.* Boulder, Colo.: Westview, 1995.

War and Culture

Cameron, Craig M. *American Samurai: Myth, Imagination, and the Conduct of Battle in the First Marine Division, 1941–1951.* Cambridge: Cambridge University Press, 1994.

Hanson, Victor Davis. *Carnage and Culture: Landmark Battles in the Rise of Western Power.* New York: Doubleday, 2001.

———. *The Western Way of War: Infantry Battle in Classical Greece.* New York: New York: Knopf, 1989.

Keegan, John. *A History of Warfare.* New York: Knopf, 1993.

Lynn, John A. *Battle: A History of Combat and Culture.* Boulder, Colo.: Westview, 2003.

Parker, Geoffrey, ed. *The Cambridge Illustrated History of Warfare: The Triumph of the West.* Cambridge: Cambridge University Press, 1995.

Poster, Patrick. "Good Anthropology, Bad History: The Cultural Turn in Studying War." *Parameters: U.S. Army War College Quarterly* 37 (Summer 2007): 45–58.

Shy, John. "The Cultural Approach to the History of War." *Journal of Military History* 57 (October 1993): 13–26.

Weigley, Russell F. *The American War of War: A History of United States Military Strategy and Practice.* Bloomington: Indiana University Press, 1973.

Military Thought

Gat, Azar. *The Origins of Military Thought: From the Enlightenment to Clausewitz.* Oxford: Oxford University Press, 1989.

Gray, Colin S. *Modern Strategy.* Oxford: Oxford University Press, 1999.

Paret, Peter. *Understanding War: Essays on Clausewitz and the History of Military Power.* Princeton: Princeton University Press, 1992.

Paret, Peter, ed. *Makers of Modern Strategy: From Machiavelli to the Nuclear Age.* Princeton: Princeton University Press, 1986.

von Clausewitz, Carl. *On War.* Translated and edited by Michael Howard and Peter Paret. Princeton: Princeton University Press, 1976.

Experience of War

Bergerud, Eric. *Touched with Fire: The Land War in the South Pacific.* New York: Penguin, 1996.

Holmes, Richard. *Acts of War: The Behavior of Men in Battle.* New York: Free Press, 1985.

———. *Redcoat: The British Soldier in the Age of Horse and Musket.* New York: Norton, 2002.

———. *Sahib: The British Soldier in India, 1750–1914.* New York: HarperCollins, 2006.

———. *Dusty Warriors: Modern Soldiers at War.* New York: HarperPerennial, 2007.

———. *Tommy: The British Soldier on the Western Front, 1914–1918.* New York: HarperCollins, 2004.

Keegan, John. *The Face of Battle: A Study of Agincourt, Waterloo, and the Somme.* New York: Vintage, 1976.

Spector, Ronald H. *At War at Sea: Sailors and Naval Combat in the Twentieth Century.* Viking, 2001.

Spiller, Roger. *An Instinct for War: Scenes from the Battlefields of History.* Cambridge: Belknap Press of Harvard University Press, 2005.

Naval History and Thought

Corbett, Julian S. *Some Principles of Maritime Strategy.* Naval Institute Press, 1972.

Finamore, Daniel, ed. *Maritime History as World History.* Gainesville: University Press of Florida, 2004.

Gray, Colin S. *The Leverage of Sea Power: The Strategic Advantage of Navies in War.* New York: Free Press, 1992.

Hattendorf, John B. *Ubi Sumus? The State of Naval and Maritime History.* Newport, R.I.: Naval War College Press, 1994.

Mahan, Alfred Thayer. *The Influence of Sea Power upon History, 1660–1763.* Boston: Little, Brown, 1890.

Padfield, Peter. *Maritime Power and the Struggle for Freedom, 1788–1851.* London: Murray, 2003.

——. *Maritime Supremacy and the Opening of the Western Mind.* New York: Overlook, 1999.

Reynolds, Clark G. *Command of the Sea: The History and Strategy of Maritime Empires.* New York: Morrow, 1974.

——. *History and the Sea: Essays on Maritime Strategies.* Columbia: University of South Carolina Press, 1989.

Rodger, N. A. M. *The Command of the Ocean: A Naval History of Britain, 1649–1815.* New York: Penguin, 2004.

Air Power

Biddle, Tami Davis. *Rhetoric and Reality in Air Warfare: The Evolution of British and American Ideas about Strategic Bombing, 1914–1945.* Princeton: Princeton University Press, 2004.

Boyne, Walter J. *The Influence of Air Power upon History.* New York: Pelican, 2003.

Buckley, John. *Air Power and the Age of Total War.* Bloomington: Indiana University Press, 1999.

Budiansky, Stephen. *Air Power.* New York: Penguin, 2003.

Cox, Sebastian, and Peter Gray, eds. *Air Power History: Turning Points from Kitty Hawk to Kosovo.* London: Cass, 2002.

Douhet, Giulio. *The Command of the Air.* Washington, D.C.: Office of Air Force History, 1983.

Gross, Charles J. *American Military Aviation: The Indispensable Arm.* College Station: Texas A&M University Press, 2002.

Hallion, Richard P., ed. *Air Power Confronts an Unstable World.* London: Brassey's, 1997.

Lambeth, Benjamin. *The Transformation of American Air Power.* Ithaca, N.Y.: Cornell University Press, 2000.

Mason, Tony. *Air Power: A Centennial Appraisal.* London: Brassey's, 1994.

War in the Global Perspective

Archer, Christon I., John R. Ferris, Holger H. Herwig, and Timothy H. E. Travers. *World History of Warfare.* Lincoln: University of Nebraska Press, 2002.

Black, Jeremy. *War and the World: Military Power and the Fate of Continents, 1450–2000.* New Haven: Yale University Press, 1998.

McNeill, William H. *The Pursuit of Power: Technology, Armed Force, and Society since A.D. 1000.* Chicago: University of Chicago Press, 1982.

Neiberg, Michael S. *Warfare in World History.* London: Routledge, 2001.

Contemporary and Future Warfare

Bacevich, Andrew. *The New American Militarism: How Americans Are Seduced by War.* Oxford: Oxford University Press, 2005.

Black, Jeremy. *War: Past, Present, and Future.* New York: St. Martin's, 2000.

Boot, Max. *The Savage Wars of Peace: Small Wars and the Rise of American Power.* New York: Basic Books, 2002.

Coker, Christopher. *The Future of War: The Re-Enchantment of War in the Twenty-First Century.* London: Blackwell, 2004.

Gray, Colin S. *Another Bloody Century: Future Warfare.* London: Cassell, 2006.

Hammes, Thomas X. *The Sling and the Stone: On War in the Twenty-First Century.* St. Paul, Minn.: Zenith, 2004.

State of Military History

Black, Jeremy. "Determinisms and Other Issues." *Journal of Military History* 68 (October 2004): 1217–32.

———. *Rethinking Military History.* London: Routledge, 2004.

Hanson, Victor Davis. "The Dilemmas of the Contemporary Military Historian." In *Reconstructing History: The Emergence of a New Historical Society,* edited by Elizabeth Fox-Genovese and Elisabeth Lasch-Quinn, 189–201. London: Routledge, 1999.

———. "The Return of Military History?" *National Review Online.* www.national review.com (July 3, 2002).

Kaplan, Robert D. "Four-Star Generalist." *Atlantic Monthly* (October 1999): 18–19.

Kennedy, Paul. "The Fall and Rise of Military History." *Military History Quarterly* 3 (Winter 1991): 9–12.

Lynn, John A. "The Embattled Future of Academic Military History." *Journal of Military History* 61 (October 1997): 777–89.

Miller, John J. "Sounding Taps: Why Military History Is Being Retired." *National Review Online.* www.nationalreview.com (October 9, 2006).

War and the Human Condition

Ferguson, Niall. *The War of the World: History's Age of Hatred.* New York: Penguin, 2006.

———. "The Next War of the World." *Foreign Affairs* 85 (September–October 2006): 61–74.

Hastings, Max. *Armageddon: The Battle for Germany, 1944–1945.* New York: Knopf, 2004.

Contributors

ANDREW J. BACEVICH is professor of international relations and history at Boston University and is the author several influential books, including *American Empire* (2004) and *The New American Militarism* (2005).

ERIC BERGERUD is professor of history at Lincoln University. He is the author of *Touched by Fire: The Land War in the South Pacific* (1996) and *Fire in the Sky: The Air War in the South Pacific* (1999).

JEREMY BLACK is professor of history at the University of Exeter, United Kingdom. He is a prolific author. Among his many books in military history are *The English Seaborne Empire* (2004), *War and the World: Military Power and the Fate of Continents, 1450–2000* (2000), and *Rethinking Military History* (2004).

MAX BOOT is senior fellow for national-security studies at the Council on Foreign Relations. He is author of the award-winning *Savage Wars of Peace: Small Wars and the Rise of American Power* (2002) and *War Made New: Technology, Warfare, and the Course of History, 1500 to Today* (2006). In 2004, he was named one of the five hundred "most influential people in the United States in the field of foreign policy" by the World Affairs Councils of America.

JEFFREY CLARKE is chief historian of the U.S. Army Center of Military History. Among his recent works is *Riviera to the Rhine,* one of the army's World War II Green Series operational histories.

ANTULIO J. ECHEVARRIA II is the director of research and director of national securities affairs at the Strategic Studies Institute, U.S. Army War College. He is author of several books including *After Clausewitz: German Military Thinkers before the Great War* (2001), *Clausewitz and Contemporary War* (2007), and *Imagining Future War* (2007).

NIALL FERGUSON is Laurence A. Tisch Professor of History at Harvard University and William Ziegler Professor of Business Administration at Harvard Business School. He is also a senior research fellow of Jesus College, Oxford University, and a senior fellow of the Hoover Institution, Stanford University. Ferguson is author of several influential books, including *The Pity of War: Explaining World War One* (1998); *Empire: The Rise and Demise of the British World Order and the Lessons for Global Power* (2003); *Colossus: The Rise and Fall of the American Empire* (2004); and most recently *The War of the World: Twentieth-Century Conflict and the Decline of the*

West (2006). In 2004 *Time* magazine named him as one of the world's hundred most influential people.

COLIN S. GRAY is a professor of international politics and strategic studies at the University of Reading, United Kingdom. He is the author of twenty-two books, including *Modern Strategy* (2000), *The Sheriff: America's Defense of the New World Order* (2004), *Another Bloody Century: Future Warfare* (2005), *Strategy and History* (2006), and *War, Peace, and International Relations: An Introduction to Strategic History* (2007).

T. X. HAMMES, Colonel USMC (Ret), is author of *The Sling and the Stone: On War in the Twenty-First Century* (2004).

VICTOR DAVIS HANSON is Martin and Illie Anderson Senior Fellow at the Hoover Institution, Stanford University, a professor emeritus at California University Fresno, and a nationally syndicated columnist. He has written numerous books, including *The Western Way of War* (1989), *The Soul of Battle* (1999), *Carnage and Culture* (2001), *Ripples of Battle* (2003), and *A War Like No Other* (2005).

MAX HASTINGS was an award-winning foreign correspondent for many years, reporting from more than sixty countries for BBC TV and the *London Evening Standard*. He was editor-in-chief of the *British Daily Telegraph* and *Evening Standard* from which he retired in 2002. He has written many books on military history and current events, including *Bomber Command* (1979), which won the Somerset Maugham Prize for nonfiction, *Overlord: D-Day and the Battle for Normandy* (1985), and *Armageddon* (2004).

RICHARD HOLMES was a member of the Department of War Studies at the Royal Military Academy Sandhurst from 1969 to 1985, when he left to command Second Battalion, the Wessex Regiment. He is now professor of military and security studies at Cranfield University, United Kingdom. He has written over twenty books on military topics, including *Acts of War: The Behavior of Men in Battle* (1986) and a trilogy on the history of the British soldier: *Redcoat* (2002), *Tommy* (2004), and *Sahib* (2005). He was general editor of *The Oxford Companion to Military History* (2001). In 1999 he became Colonel of the Princess of Wales's Royal Regiment, and his book *Dusty Warriors* (2006) considers his First Battalion tour of duty in Iraq in 2004.

PETER PARET is professor emeritus at the Institute for Advanced Study. His principal interests are the history of art and culture and the history of war. In the latter field he has written, among other works, *Clausewitz and the State* (1976) and a volume of essays *Understanding War* (1992). He edited *Makers of Modern Strategy* (1986) and with Michael Howard translated and edited Clausewitz's *On War* (1976). He gave the 2008 Lee Knowles Lectures in the History of War at Cambridge University.

GEOFFREY PARKER is Andreas Dorpalen Professor of History at Ohio State University and a Fellow of the British Academy. He is the author of many important books in military history, including the award-winning *The Military Revolution. Military Innovation and the Rise of the West, 1500–1800* (1988), *The Grand Strategy of Philip II* (1998), and *The Thirty Years' War* (1997).

Dennis Showalter is professor of history at Colorado College and a past president of the Society for Military History. His *Tannenberg: Clash of Empires* (1991) won the Paul Birdsall Prize.

Donald A. Yerxa is editor of *Historically Speaking* and professor of history at Eastern Nazarene College. He is the author of three books, including *Admirals and Empire* (1991). He has interviewed scores of historians for several publications.

Index